PAUL DUNN

Switching On Your Brand

Marketing for Tradespeople

Copyright © 2024 by Paul Dunn

Copyright ©2024 by Paul Dunn. All rights reserved. No part of this book may be reproduced, stored in a retrieval system, or transmitted in any form or by any means—electronic, mechanical, photocopying, recording, or otherwise—without prior written permission from the author or publisher, except for brief quotations used in reviews or critical articles.

This book is published by P. D. Electrical, with the intent of sharing general insights, strategies, and guidance for electricians, tradespeople, and small business owners. The content is provided for informational and educational purposes only.

The author and publisher make no representations or warranties with respect to the accuracy, applicability, or completeness of the content within this book. The strategies, techniques, and advice outlined are based on the author's experiences and research, but individual results may vary.

This book is not intended to serve as financial, legal, or professional advice. The reader is encouraged to consult with appropriate professionals before implementing any suggestions or recommendations. The author and publisher disclaim any liability or responsibility for any losses, damages, or consequences—financial or otherwise—that may result from the use or misuse of the information contained in this book.

All trademarks, logos, and brand names referenced in this book are the property of their respective owners. Their inclusion does not imply endorsement or affiliation.

Printed in the United Kingdom.

First edition

This book was professionally typeset on Reedsy.
Find out more at reedsy.com

Contents

INTRODUCTION	1
BUILDING A BRAND THAT SPARKS ATTENTION	4
MASTERING YOUR ONLINE PRESENCE	18
ATTRACTING YOUR DREAM CLIENTS	33
THE POWER OF CONTENT MARKETING	48
WINNING AT CUSTOMER RETENTION	62
SCALING WITHOUT LOSING YOUR TOUCH	77
STANDING OUT IN A COMPETITIVE MARKET	92
TURNING REVIEWS INTO REVENUE	106
MARKETING ON A SHOESTRING BUDGET	121
FUTURE-PROOFING YOUR ELECTRICAL BUSINESS	136
POWERING UP YOUR FUTURE: THE NEXT STEP TO UNSTOPPABLE GROWTH	151
About the Author	156
Also by Paul Dunn	158

INTRODUCTION

Hi, I'm Paul Dunn, and I appreciate you picking up this book.

I've been an electrician for over 20 years and have experienced first-hand the challenges of running a business in the trades. You're juggling jobs, keeping clients happy, and trying to stand out in a market flooded with competition—all while ensuring the work you do meets the highest standards. Like you, I'm not a marketer. I'm just someone who's had to figure out how to build a business that works, often through trial and error.

I know what it's like to:

- Spend hours trying to stand out, only to feel like your business is invisible in a crowded marketplace.
- Watch clients pick the cheapest option while you're left wondering how to get paid what you're worth.
- Feel stuck working with difficult clients who haggle over every penny and still aren't satisfied.
- Scramble for jobs during slow periods, taking on work you'd rather avoid just to keep the cash flow going.

Sound familiar? You're not alone.

The truth is, the problem isn't your skills or your work ethic—it's how your business is positioned and how you communicate your value to the right clients. Without clear strategies, it's easy to get caught in a frustrating cycle:

The Drought: The phone's not ringing, and the jobs aren't coming in. You feel stuck, questioning what you're doing wrong.

The Scramble: In desperation, you lower your rates or take on less-than-ideal jobs to make ends meet, even though it leaves you overworked and underpaid.

The Burnout: The long hours and constant stress take a toll. You're frustrated, exhausted, and wondering if it's even worth it.

The Quick Fix: You throw money at solutions like ads or websites that promise quick results but fail to deliver.

The False Dawn: A couple of decent clients come through, and you think things are improving—until the cycle starts all over again.

If this sounds all too familiar, it's time to break free.

This book is designed to help you step out of the grind and build a business that attracts high-quality clients who value what you do and are willing to pay for it. It's not about flashy marketing or gimmicks—it's about using practical strategies that fit who you are as a trades-person and business owner. While the examples in this book are aimed at electricians, the principles and strategies shared can apply to all tradespeople, providing a solid foundation for anyone looking to elevate their trade business.

By the time you finish, you'll have the tools and confidence to:

- Establish a strong, trusted reputation in your market.
- Attract clients who respect your expertise and pay what you're worth.
- Build systems that keep your business running smoothly and profitably.

This isn't about working harder—it's about working smarter, making the most of what you already bring to the table. You've mastered your trade; now it's time to master the business side.

Let's get started.

BUILDING A BRAND THAT SPARKS ATTENTION

DEFINING YOUR BRAND IDENTITY

Your business is more than just electrical work. It's you. It's how you answer the phone, the way you show up to a job, and even the way you leave a site at the end of the day. Your brand is the sum total of all these impressions, and it's what sets you apart from the bloke down the road charging £20 less. If you can nail down your brand identity, you'll attract more of the customers you want and less of the tyre-kickers who waste your time. Let's break this down into three key areas: your unique value, your logo and tag-line, and your brand colours.

Your Unique Value as an Electrician (and Beyond)

There are thousands of electricians (and tradespeople) out there, but none of them are you. Your unique value is what makes you different, and it's what convinces a customer to choose you over someone else. Start by asking yourself:

What do I do better than anyone else? Maybe you're incredibly tidy—your work van is organised better than a Swiss watch factory, and your job sites are left spotless. Maybe you specialise in a specific niche like smart home installations or energy-efficient systems.

Whatever it is, own it. Write it down in clear, simple terms. If you're struggling to pinpoint it, think about what your best customers have said about you. Did they rave about your reliability? Your creative problem-solving? Your ability to explain complicated electrical jargon in a way that makes sense? That's your edge. That's your unique value.

Once you've identified this, everything else in your brand should reflect it. If your edge is being the go-to expert for electric vehicle (EV) charging stations, your website, business cards, and even your social media posts should scream that. Don't try to be everything to everyone. The trades-person who tries to do it all ends up being remembered for nothing.

Creating a Memorable Logo and Tag-line

Let's talk logos. A logo is not just a random design you slap on your van. It's a visual handshake—a silent first impression that speaks volumes about your professionalism. A good logo is clean, simple, and easy to recognise. Don't overcomplicate it with too many colours or fussy details. Think about iconic brands like Nike or McDonald's. Their logos are simple yet powerful.

As an electrician, you'll want something that subtly communicates the nature of your work. A lightning bolt, a plug, or a wire motif can work well, but avoid clichés that make your business blend into the background. Hire a professional designer if you can afford it. If not, there are affordable tools like Canva or online freelancers who can create something polished on a budget.

Now, your tag-line. This is your chance to sum up your unique value in a sentence or less. It should be memorable and customer-focused. For example: - "Powering Homes, Empowering Lives." - "Reliable Electrical Solutions, Every Time." - "Your Local Expert for Smarter Energy."

A great tag-line not only reinforces what you do but also how you do it. Don't just say, 'We do electrical work.' That's boring and vague. Make it about the customer and their experience when they choose you.

Choosing Brand Colours That Resonate

Colours are more powerful than you think. They trigger emotions, create associations, and influence how people perceive your business. The right colour palette can make the difference between looking like a cheap DIY operation or a premium professional service.

In the trades, blue is a classic choice because it conveys trust, reliability, and professionalism. Think banks, insurance companies, and yes, trades businesses. Blue says, 'You can trust me to do the job right.' If you want to stand out a bit, consider complementary colours like grey, orange, or even a bold yellow.

Whatever colours you choose, keep it consistent across everything—your van, your uniforms, your website, and even your invoices. Consistency builds recognition. If someone sees your van parked on a street and then spots your flyer later, they should instantly connect the two.

Avoid using too many colours, as that can make your brand look messy or amateurish. Stick to two or three primary colours and use them strategically. For instance, your main colour (say, blue) could be the background for your business cards, while a secondary colour (like grey) could be used for text or accents.

And here's a practical tip: make sure your colours look good on both digital screens and printed material. What looks sleek on your website might not translate well to a van wrap or uniform. Always test it out before committing.

When you define your brand identity with clarity and purpose, you're laying the foundation for everything else in your business. It's not just about looking good—it's about creating an experience for your customers that feels professional, trustworthy, and uniquely yours.

POSITIONING YOURSELF AS THE GO-TO EXPERT

Picture this: a homeowner's power goes out in the middle of dinner prep, or a small business owner's security lights suddenly fail during a busy week. Who do they call first? The electrician they trust. The one they know will show up, do the job right, and leave them feeling like they just got the VIP treatment. That's who you need to be—the go-to expert. You're not just an option. You're the option.

But how do you get there? How do you climb to the top of the list in your community or niche? Simple: you position yourself as the authority, the trusted professional, the one they don't just need but actually prefer. Let's get into how you can make that happen.

Identifying Your Niche Market

Here's the thing: you can't be everything to everyone. Let's say you're an electrician who tries to do it all—domestic, commercial, industrial, solar, rewiring, smart homes, EV charging stations, and even the odd ceiling fan installation. Sure, you might pick up a few jobs here and there, but you'll blend in with every other "generalist" out there. And in a competitive market, blending in is a recipe for invisibility.

Instead, think about narrowing your focus. Ask yourself: What do I enjoy doing the most? and What's in high demand in my area? Maybe you're brilliant at installing EV chargers, or you've got a knack for solving complex electrical faults in older homes. When you identify a niche—something you can specialise in—you stop being a jack-of-all-trades and start being a master of one. And people pay more for the master.

Say you choose smart home technology as your niche. Homeowners will remember you as the person who turned their house into a fully automated dream. Or maybe you focus on small commercial spaces. You become the go-to for local shops, cafés, and offices that need seamless electrical solutions.

By specialising, you carve out a space where competition thins out and customers come specifically to you because they know you're the best at that one thing. You're no longer competing with every electrician in town; you're standing in your own lane.

Establishing Authority Through Expertise

So, you've picked your niche. Now it's time to prove you know your stuff. Because let's face it, people don't just want to hire someone who can do the job—they want someone who inspires confidence. They want to feel like they're in safe, capable hands. That's where your expertise comes in.

Start by sharing your knowledge with the world. This doesn't mean you have to give away your trade secrets for free, but it does mean you need to demonstrate that you're not just skilled—you're an expert. Write a quick blog post or make a short video explaining something practical, like "How to Choose the Right EV Charger for Your Home" or "5 Signs Your Wiring Needs an Upgrade." Don't overthink it; just talk about what you already know.

You can also share tips on social media. Imagine a homeowner scrolling through Facebook and stumbling upon your 30-second video explaining why surge protectors are a must for modern homes. Not only are you educating them, but you're also planting a seed: This person knows what they're talking about. I should call them when I need help.

Another way to establish authority? Get certified in your niche. If you're diving into solar installations, for instance, take the extra time to get accredited by a recognised organisation. Certifications aren't just for show—they're proof that you're serious about your craft. And when customers see those badges on your website or van, they'll know you're not just winging it.

Don't underestimate the power of testimonials, either. Ask satisfied clients to vouch for your expertise. When someone says, "This electrician saved me thousands by identifying an issue no one else could," it's like gold dust for your reputation. People trust people, and social proof is one of the fastest ways to establish yourself as the authority in your niche.

Communicating Trust and Reliability

Let's be real: trust is the cornerstone of any great tradesperson-client relationship. If your customers don't trust you, they're not calling you back. Worse, they're not recommending you to their friends. So how do you build that trust? By being reliable, transparent, and professional at every touch point.

It starts with your first interaction—whether that's a phone call, an email, or a message via your website. Respond quickly and clearly. If someone leaves you a voicemail, call them back as soon as you can. If they email, reply within a day. Even a simple "Hey, thanks for reaching out! I'll get back to you by [insert time]" beats radio silence. People remember when you respect their time.

When you do show up to a job, look the part. Your uniform doesn't have to be fancy, but it should be clean. Your van doesn't need to be brand-new, but it should be tidy and professional-looking. These little details send a big message: I take my work seriously.

Clear communication is another trust-builder. Before you start a job, walk your client through what you're going to do and why. No one likes surprises when it comes to their bill, so be upfront about costs and timelines. If something changes mid-job, let them know immediately. People appreciate honesty, even if it's not always what they want to hear.

Here's a pro tip: always leave a job cleaner than you found it.

It might seem minor, but leaving behind a spotless workspace shows respect for your client's property. It's a small gesture that makes a big impact.

Finally, stand by your work. Offer guarantees where you can. For example, "If anything goes wrong with this installation in the next year, I'll come back and fix it for free." That's a bold statement, but it tells your customers you're confident in your skills—and it gives them peace of mind.

So, how do you become the go-to expert in your community or niche? You specialise, you demonstrate expertise, and you build trust through reliability and professionalism. It's not about being flashy or over-the-top; it's about showing up as the best version of yourself and delivering value consistently. Before you know it, your name will be the one people think of first when they need an electrician they can count on.

CRAFTING YOUR BRAND STORY

Your story is your superpower. It's what sets you apart from every other electrician or trades-person in your area. People don't just hire a service; they hire a person, a trust, and a connection. Your brand story is the bridge that connects you to your customers on a deeper level, turning a simple transaction into a relationship that lasts. So, how do you craft a story that makes people remember your name and choose you over the competition? Let's break it down.

Sharing Your Journey Authentically

Your journey is where it all begins. Whether you started as an apprentice straight out of school or spent years working for someone else before going solo, your path has shaped who you are and how you do business. Don't underestimate the power of sharing it. Customers want to know the person behind the service—they want to feel like they're hiring someone they can trust, not just ticking a box.

Start by asking yourself: Why did you become an electrician? What drove you to start your own business? Maybe you grew up watching your dad fix things around the house, and you've always had a knack for making things work. Maybe you saw an opportunity to bring better customer service to a trade that's often criticised for being unreliable. Whatever it is, write it down. Keep it real and avoid the temptation to embellish. Authenticity is what resonates with people.

Think about the moments that shaped your journey. Was there a time when you went above and beyond for a client, and it made you realise how much of an impact your work has? Share those moments. They're the kinds of stories that stick with people. They show that you're not just another electrician—you're someone who genuinely cares about the work and the people you serve.

Your journey doesn't have to be dramatic or extraordinary to be compelling. It just has to be real. When you tell it as it is, your audience will feel it. And when they feel it, they'll trust you. And trust? That's the foundation of every successful business.

Connecting Emotionally with Customers

People make decisions based on emotion first and logic second. This is true whether they're deciding what to eat for dinner or who to call when their fuse box is on the fritz. If you want to stand out, you need to connect emotionally with your customers. Your story is the gateway to that connection.

Think about your ideal customer. What keeps them up at night? Maybe it's the fear of hiring someone who won't show up on time or will leave the job half-done. Maybe it's the stress of dealing with an unexpected electrical issue that's thrown their whole day into chaos. Your story should speak to those fears and frustrations—not as a sales pitch, but as a way of showing that you get it. You're not just an electrician; you're someone who understands what they're going through and can help solve their problems with professionalism and care.

Take the time to weave in the values that matter most to your customers. Do you pride yourself on being punctual? Do you prioritise safety above all else? Do you treat every home or workspace like it's your own? These are the things that build trust and loyalty, and they should come through in your story naturally.

It's not just about what you say; it's about how you say it. Use language that feels human and approachable. Avoid jargon that might confuse or alienate your audience. Instead, speak to them like you would a neighbour or a friend. When you strip away the formalities, you create a connection that feels personal and genuine.

Remember, your customers aren't just hiring you for your technical skills. They're hiring you because they believe you'll make their lives easier, not harder. Your story should reflect that. It should show that you're not just a trades-person—you're a partner they can rely on.

Keeping Your Story Consistent Across Channels

Once you've nailed down your story, the next step is making sure it's consistent across every touchpoint of your business. Your website, social media profiles, Google My Business page, business cards, and even the way you introduce yourself to potential clients—it all needs to tell the same story.

Consistency isn't just about repeating the same words over and over again. It's about creating a cohesive image of who you are and what you stand for. If someone visits your website and sees a professional, approachable brand, but then checks out your social media and finds a bunch of unrelated memes or poorly written posts, that disconnect can erode trust. Your story should feel seamless, no matter where or how people come across your business.

Start with your website. This is often the first place potential customers will go to learn about you. Your "About" page is your opportunity to share your story in a way that feels personal and relatable. Skip the corporate-speak and focus on what makes you, you. Use photos of yourself and your team to put a face to the name—it's a simple way to make your story feel more real and human.

On social media, your story should come through in the tone of your posts, the types of content you share, and even the way you interact with followers. If your story is about being a reliable, community-focused electrician, then your posts should reflect that. Share behind-the-scenes looks at your work, highlight customer success stories, and engage with local events or causes. Every post is an opportunity to reinforce your story and build connections.

Don't forget about offline channels, too. Your business cards, van signage, and even the way you answer the phone should all align with the story you're telling. If your brand is all about professionalism and reliability, make sure your printed materials and interactions reflect that. A clean, well-designed business card says a lot about your attention to detail, just like showing up in a tidy, branded uniform speaks volumes about your commitment to quality.

Here's the thing: consistency builds trust. When people see the same story playing out across every interaction they have with your business, it reinforces the idea that you're exactly who you say you are. And when they trust you, they're far more likely to choose you—and recommend you to others.

Your brand story isn't just a nice-to-have; it's a powerful tool for building trust, creating emotional connections, and setting yourself apart in a competitive market. By sharing your journey authentically, speaking to what matters most to your customers, and keeping your story consistent across every channel, you'll create a brand that people remember—and a business that thrives.

MASTERING YOUR ONLINE PRESENCE

BUILDING A WEBSITE THAT CONVERTS

Your website is your digital store front. It's the first impression many of your clients will have of you, even before they pick up the phone or send an email. And just like you wouldn't let your physical workspace stay cluttered or unprofessional, your website shouldn't be a half-done afterthought. A website that works isn't just about looking good; it's about converting visitors into paying customers.

User-Friendly Design Essentials

Think about the last time you visited a website that frustrated you. Maybe it was hard to navigate, took forever to load, or you couldn't find the basic info you needed. You didn't stick around, did you? That's exactly what your potential clients will do if your website isn't user-friendly.

Start with simplicity. Don't try to cram everything onto your homepage. A clean, uncluttered design with clear navigation is what you're aiming for. Your menu should be straightforward: Home, About, Services, Reviews, Blog (if you have one), and Contact. That's it. Resist the urge to be fancy with weird fonts or flashy animations that slow down the page. Keep it professional, but approachable.

Mobile responsiveness is non-negotiable. Over 70% of web traffic now comes from mobile devices. If your website looks like a distorted mess on a phone, you're losing business. Test it yourself: pull up your site on a phone and tablet. Is everything easy to read? Are buttons and links easy to tap? If not, it's time to talk to your web developer or explore platforms like WordPress or Squarespace that have mobile-friendly templates built in.

Also, speed matters. Your potential client isn't going to wait 10 seconds for your site to load while they're on their lunch break. Compress images, clean up unused plug-ins, and make sure your hosting provider isn't slowing you down. A good rule of thumb: your site should load in under three seconds.

Crafting Service Pages That Sell

Your service pages aren't just there to list what you do; they're there to sell what you do. When someone clicks on "Electrical Services" or "Commercial Wiring," they're not looking for poetry. They're looking for answers.

Start each service page with a short, punchy headline that makes it clear how you'll solve the customer's problem. For example, instead of "Residential Electrical Services," try "Safe, Reliable Wiring for Your Home – Every Time." This immediately communicates value and builds trust.

Break your services into sections with clear subheadings. Use bullet points to outline specifics, like "Fuse Box Upgrades," "Outdoor Lighting Installation," or "Emergency Call-outs." This makes it easy for people to scan the page and find what they need.

Here's a tip: don't just describe what you do—explain why it matters to them. For example, instead of saying, "We install ceiling fans," say, "Stay cool and save on energy bills with professionally installed ceiling fans." You're not selling the service; you're selling the outcome.

Include real photos of your work. Stock images don't cut it any more. A potential client wants to see the lighting system you installed at a local business or the tidy wiring job you did in someone's loft. And if you can add a caption explaining what the job was and where it's located, even better.

Finally, don't forget proof. Include testimonials or mini case studies right on the service pages. A small quote like, "John fixed our flickering lights in no time—highly recommend!" can tip a hesitant visitor into becoming a paying customer.

Integrating Call-to-Actions That Work

If you've ever been on a website and thought, "What do I do next?" the site failed you. Don't make that mistake. Every page on your website should have a clear call-to-action (CTA) that tells the visitor exactly what step to take.

Your CTAs need to stand out. Use contrasting colours for buttons, and place them in logical spots—at the top of the page, after key sections, and at the bottom. Make them action-oriented. Instead of a button that says "Submit," try "Request a Free Quote" or "Book Your Service Now." These are specific and encourage immediate action.

Think about offering something valuable in exchange for their contact info. A free consultation, an estimate, or even a downloadable guide like "5 Warning Signs Your Home Needs Electrical Maintenance." This not only builds trust but gets them into your pipeline for follow-up.

Don't overlook the importance of contact forms. Keep them simple. Ask for their name, email, phone number, and a brief description of their issue. Anything more, and they'll click away. And test your forms regularly—there's nothing worse than a potential lead filling out a form that never reaches your inbox.

Another key is having your phone number visible at all times. Place it in the top right-hand corner of your site where it's easy to spot. Make it clickable for mobile users so they can call you with one tap. Accessibility equals conversions.

Lastly, add a live chat feature if possible. Many potential clients prefer texting over calling these days, especially for non-urgent inquiries. There are affordable chat tools available that you can manage right from your phone. It's a small touch that can make a big difference in how professional and responsive you appear.

Your website isn't just a static brochure—it's a 24/7 salesperson working on your behalf. When done right, it doesn't just bring people in; it turns them into loyal clients.

LEVERAGING GOOGLE FOR MAXIMUM VISIBILITY

If you're not leveraging Google to its fullest potential, you're leaving money on the table. Whether you're rewiring a Victorian home or installing a fancy smart thermostat in a new build, your potential clients are searching for someone just like you on Google. The question is, are they finding you or your competition? Here's how to make sure you're the one they call.

Setting Up and Optimising Google My Business

Your Google My Business (GMB) profile is like a digital handshake. It's often the first thing people see when they Google "electrician near me" or "emergency electrical repair." If you don't have a GMB profile yet, stop whatever you're doing and set one up. It's free, and it's the single most important tool for getting found locally online.

When setting it up, don't skip any steps. Add your business name exactly as it appears on your website and other listings (consistency is key here). Include your address, phone number, and business hours. Make sure your service area is clearly defined—whether you cover just your town, the wider county, or beyond.

Next, upload high-quality photos that showcase your work. Think: a clean and organised van, your team in branded uniforms, and shots of completed projects like a newly installed consumer unit or a sparkling LED lighting setup. People want to see what you're all about before they give you a call, so these visuals are your first opportunity to build trust.

Don't underestimate the power of your business description either. You have 750 characters to sell yourself—use them wisely. Make it clear what you specialise in and what makes you different. "Reliable electrician serving Bath and surrounding areas. Specialists in EV charger installation, smart home tech, and emergency repairs." You're not just an electrician; you're the electrician people can count on.

Finally, keep your GMB profile fresh. Update it with new photos, special offers, or seasonal services. If you're offering a discount on outdoor lighting installations for summer or promoting portable generator setups ahead of winter, let people know. Google loves activity on GMB, and so do potential customers.

Ranking Higher with Local SEO

Ranking on Google isn't just about having a great GMB profile—it's also about what's happening on your website and across the web. Local SEO (Search Engine Optimisation) is your ticket to showing up higher in search results.

Start with the basics: keywords. These are the words and phrases people type into Google when they're looking for someone like you. Think "emergency electrician in Manchester" or "fuse box replacement near me." Sprinkle these keywords naturally throughout your website—on your homepage, service pages, and even blog posts.

Your website's "About" and "Contact" pages are gold mines for local SEO. Make sure your location is prominent. If you cover multiple areas, list them. For example: "We proudly serve Leeds, Bradford, and the surrounding areas." This way, Google knows where to show your business to searchers.

Next, get your business listed in local directories. Sites like Yelp, Yell, and Checkatrade are not only places where customers look for tradespeople, but they also boost your SEO. Make sure your NAP (Name, Address, Phone number) is consistent across all platforms. Google hates inconsistency, and it could knock you down the rankings.

Backlinks are another powerhouse for local SEO. These are links from other websites that point to yours. Partner with local businesses or organisations to get featured on their websites.

Maybe a builder you've worked with can add a shout-out to your services on their "Trusted Partners" page. Or perhaps you can sponsor a local youth football team and get your business linked on their site.

And don't ignore mobile optimisation. A massive chunk of searches for tradespeople happens on phones. Your website needs to load quickly and look great on smaller screens. If someone's standing in their kitchen with a broken light fixture, they're not going to wait around for your site to load—they'll move on to the next search result.

Getting More Reviews That Matter

Reviews can make or break your online presence. They're not just about ego-boosting 5-star ratings (although those do feel great). Reviews are a trust signal for new customers and a ranking factor for Google. In short, they're crucial.

The best way to get reviews? Ask. After you finish a job, don't just collect your tools and head out the door. Take a moment to thank your customer and say something like, "If you're happy with the work, I'd really appreciate it if you could leave a quick review on Google. It helps people find me and lets them know they can trust my services." Make it easy for them by sending a follow-up text or email with a direct link to your review page.

Timing is everything here. Ask while the job is still fresh in their mind—before they've had a chance to get distracted by the rest of their day.

But don't stop at just collecting reviews. Respond to every single one. For positive reviews, a quick "Thanks, John! It was a pleasure helping you with your kitchen lighting upgrade" is enough. For negative reviews, stay calm and professional. Address the issue, apologise if necessary, and offer a solution. Something like, "We're sorry to hear you weren't satisfied with the service. Please contact us directly so we can make it right." How you handle criticism says a lot about your business, and potential customers are watching.

One thing to avoid: fake reviews. It might be tempting to ask friends or family to leave glowing feedback, but Google is getting smarter at spotting fakes. If you're caught, it could harm your rankings—or worse, your reputation.

Reviews aren't just for Google either. Make the most of them by featuring standout testimonials on your website and social media. A photo of a happy customer next to their glowing review adds credibility and shows potential clients that you're the real deal.

By setting up and optimising your GMB profile, focusing on local SEO, and building a steady stream of genuine reviews, you'll make Google work for you instead of the other way around. When someone in your area needs an electrician, you'll be the name they see—and the one they trust.

SOCIAL MEDIA FOR ELECTRICIANS

Choosing the Right Platforms

You don't need to be everywhere, but you do need to be where your customers are. Not every social media platform is created equal, especially for tradespeople like electricians. You're not trying to go viral with dance trends or memes; you're trying to connect with homeowners, property managers, and business owners who need your expertise. So, where do you start?

Facebook should be at the top of your list. It's the neighbourhood noticeboard of the internet. People go there to ask for recommendations, check reviews, and get a feel for local businesses. It's where your future customers are likely to search for "electrician near me" or post in community groups asking, "Does anyone know a good sparky?" If you're not there, you're missing out on conversations that could be leading directly to your next job.

Instagram comes next, especially if your work is highly visual. Think about it: before-and-after shots of a rewired kitchen, a stunning lighting install, or even the chaos you walked into before you worked your magic. These images can tell a story about the quality and professionalism of your work. And let's not forget Instagram Stories and Reels. These quick, engaging formats are perfect for showing off your skills and personality in bite-sized chunks.

LinkedIn might seem like the odd one out, but think of it as your digital business card for networking with other professionals. Builders, contractors, and property managers are all there, sharing projects and looking for reliable tradespeople to collaborate with. If you're aiming to expand your commercial client base, LinkedIn could be a goldmine.

Then there's TikTok. You might think it's just for kids, but tradespeople are carving out a niche there by showing off their skills in short, snappy videos. A quick "how to reset your fuse box" clip or a time-lapse of a tricky install? Those can attract attention from curious viewers who, when the time comes, will remember the electrician who made the complicated stuff look simple.

Posting Content That Engages

Social media isn't about shouting into the void; it's about starting conversations. The more you engage your audience, the more likely they are to think of you when they need help. So what kind of content works for electricians?

First off, educate your audience. You might take it for granted that everyone knows the difference between a breaker and a fuse, but they don't. Post quick tips like "How to know if it's time to upgrade your home's wiring" or "Why you should never ignore flickering lights." These kinds of posts position you as the expert while also being genuinely helpful.

Behind-the-scenes content is another winner. Show people what a day in your life looks like. Maybe it's a time-lapse of you rewiring a junction box or a quick selfie video explaining how you fixed a client's faulty outdoor lighting. This isn't just about showing off your skills; it's about humanising your brand. People hire people, not faceless companies.

Customer success stories can also be powerful. Did you recently help a family with an emergency repair that saved their weekend? Did you upgrade someone's home to energy-efficient lighting, cutting their bills in half? Share these stories (with your client's permission, of course). Pair them with before-and-after photos or videos for maximum impact.

Don't underestimate the power of reviews and testimonials. A simple post that says, "Thanks to [Client Name] for this lovely review!" paired with their feedback can work wonders for building trust. It's social proof that you're reliable, professional, and worth hiring.

And don't forget to inject a bit of personality into your posts. Share your thoughts on the latest industry trends, tell a funny (non-technical) story from your week, or celebrate a milestone like completing a big project or hitting a certain number of happy customers. People want to see the human side of your business, not just the technical side.

Using Paid Ads Effectively

Organic reach on social media can only take you so far. If you want to supercharge your visibility, it's time to dip your toe into paid ads. But don't worry; you don't need a massive budget to make an impact. Even a small investment can yield big results if you do it right.

Start with Facebook Ads. It's one of the most cost-effective platforms, and its targeting options are ridiculously specific. You can narrow down your audience by location, age, interests, and even behaviours. For example, you could target homeowners within a 20-mile radius who've shown interest in home improvement. That's your ideal customer, right?

When creating ads, focus on solving a specific problem. A headline like "Lights Flickering? We'll Fix It Fast!" or "Upgrade to Energy-Efficient Lighting and Cut Your Bills" speaks directly to your audience's needs. Pair it with an eye-catching image or video – maybe a clip of you in action or a before-and-after shot of your work.

Don't forget about retargeting ads. These are ads that show up for people who've already interacted with your business, like visiting your website or engaging with one of your posts. They're a gentle nudge that says, "Hey, remember us? We're still here to help."

Instagram Ads work similarly, but they're more visual. If you're already posting high-quality photos of your work, you're halfway there. Turn those posts into ads by targeting local users who might need an electrician. And don't just stick to static images; videos and Stories Ads can be incredibly engaging. Imagine a quick clip showing how you transformed a dull living room into a cosy, well-lit space – that's the kind of stuff that stops people mid-scroll.

LinkedIn Ads can be pricier, but if your goal is to land big commercial contracts, they're worth considering. Focus on targeting decision-makers like property managers, project managers, or business owners. A sponsored post highlighting a recent commercial project you've completed could catch their eye.

Whatever platform you choose, always include a clear call-to-action in your ads. Whether it's "Call Now for a Free Quote," "Message Us to Learn More," or "Visit Our Website to Book Today," make it easy for people to take the next step.

Finally, track your results. All major social media platforms offer analytics tools that show how your ads are performing. Pay attention to metrics like clicks, impressions, and conversions. If something's not working, tweak your approach. A great ad campaign isn't set-it-and-forget-it; it's an ongoing experiment.

Social media isn't just for selfies and cat videos. It's a powerful tool for electricians who want to connect with their community, showcase their expertise, and grow their business. When you pick the right platforms, post engaging content, and invest wisely in ads, you'll find yourself not just keeping up with the competition but leading the charge.

ATTRACTING YOUR DREAM CLIENTS

UNDERSTANDING YOUR TARGET AUDIENCE

Let's get to the heart of it: you can't attract your dream clients if you don't know who they are. This isn't about guessing or relying on vague stereotypes about homeowners or builders. It's about getting crystal clear on who they are, what keeps them up at night, and how you can step in to solve their problems. When you understand your audience inside out, your marketing efforts stop feeling like darts thrown in the dark. Instead, you'll have a laser-focused approach that speaks directly to the clients you want to serve.

Creating Detailed Customer Profiles

If you haven't already, it's time to build your customer profiles. No, this isn't something reserved for big corporations with endless resources. It's a tool that can transform how you approach your business, no matter the size. Start by asking yourself:

1. Who are the clients I most enjoy working with?
2. What kinds of jobs do I find most profitable?
3. What types of customers value my work and pay on time without haggling?

Your answers will give you a starting point. Let's say you're an electrician who enjoys working on high-end residential properties. Your ideal customer might be a homeowner who values quality and aesthetics, is willing to spend on premium finishes, and appreciates clear communication. Or maybe you prefer commercial work, which means your dream client could be a small business owner who needs reliable electrical systems to avoid downtime.

Take it a step further and flesh out their demographics: age, location, income level, job roles. Then dig deeper into psychographics – what motivates them, what they worry about, and what they expect from a trades-person like you. If you're targeting homeowners, think about their concerns: "Will this electrician be reliable?" "Will they leave my home tidy?" "Will they overcharge me?"

Once you've established these profiles, give them names. For instance, "Meticulous Mary" might be the homeowner who wants a flawless finish and doesn't mind paying for it. Or "Busy Ben" could be the property manager who needs someone who can get the job done quickly and without drama. By naming them, you humanise your audience and start to see them as real people rather than abstract ideas.

Understanding Pain Points and Solutions

Now that you know who you're talking to, it's time to focus on what keeps them awake at night. Pain points aren't just minor annoyances; they're the problems that make your clients feel stressed, frustrated, or even angry. Your job is to figure out what these are and position yourself as the solution.

For example, homeowners might be worried about safety ("Is my wiring up to code?"), convenience ("Will this project disrupt my family's routine?"), or cost ("Am I getting ripped off?"). Small business owners might care about reliability ("Can I count on this electrician to show up when promised?") and speed ("How quickly can they get my lights back on so I can reopen my shop?").

Once you've identified the pain points, craft your messaging around how you solve them. Address these concerns directly in your marketing materials. For instance:

- "All work is guaranteed to meet or exceed UK safety standards."
- "We show up on time and finish on schedule – no exceptions."
- "Transparent pricing means no surprises on your invoice."

When you speak directly to their fears and frustrations, you're not just selling a service – you're offering peace of mind. That's what makes you stand out in a crowded market.

One useful hack is to ask your existing clients what they care about most. A quick follow-up call or email after completing a job can reveal gold. You might learn that your clients love how you explain things clearly or how you keep the worksite pristine. Use that feedback to fine-tune your messaging and highlight what really matters to them.

Tailoring Your Marketing Message

Now that you've got a clear picture of your ideal clients and their pain points, it's time to adjust how you communicate. Generic marketing won't do. Your messaging needs to feel like it was written just for them.

Think about the tone and language you use. If you're targeting homeowners, keep it friendly, approachable, and easy to understand. Avoid technical jargon – they don't care about the complicated details of electrical systems; they care about safety, aesthetics, and functionality. On the other hand, if you're marketing to builders or contractors, they might appreciate a more professional tone and details about your technical expertise or the brands of materials you use.

Your visuals matter too. A clean, modern website with high-quality photos of your work will appeal to homeowners, while builders might be more impressed by case studies or testimonials from other professionals in the industry.

Consistency is key. Whether it's your website, social media, or even the way you answer the phone, your message should always reinforce who you are and how you solve your clients' problems. Think of it as having a conversation with your dream client: everything you say and do should make them think, "This person gets me. They're exactly who I need."

Don't forget to highlight what sets you apart. Maybe it's your 24/7 emergency service, your eco-friendly practices, or your extensive experience in a specific niche. Whatever it is, make it front and centre in your marketing.

Finally, don't be afraid to experiment. Try different approaches and see what resonates. Run an ad with a specific message and track how many leads it generates. Post different types of content on social media and see which gets the most engagement. Over time, you'll refine your messaging and discover what really works to attract your dream clients.

When you deeply understand your target audience, everything else becomes easier. Your marketing feels natural, your messaging hits home, and the clients you truly want to work with start coming to you. It's not magic – it's the power of knowing exactly who you're talking to and speaking their language.

DESIGNING YOUR IDEAL CUSTOMER JOURNEY

You know that feeling when a job goes smoothly from start to finish, and the client is so happy they're already planning to recommend you to their friends? That's not luck – that's the result of a well-thought-out customer journey. When you map out every step your customer takes – from the first time they hear about you to the day they leave you a glowing review – you take control of how your business is perceived and experienced. This isn't just about doing good work; it's about making every interaction seamless, enjoyable, and worth talking about. Let's break it down.

Mapping Out the Sales Funnel

Think of your customer journey as a funnel. At the top, you've got people who are just becoming aware of your business. They've got a problem – maybe their lights keep flickering, or they need a complete rewiring – and they're looking for someone to fix it. That's where you come in. Your job is to guide them from "Who should I call?" to "I'm booking this electrician right now."

Start with the awareness stage. How are people finding you? Maybe it's a Google search, a recommendation from a builder, or a post they scrolled past on social media. Whatever it is, make sure your messaging is clear and consistent. If someone visits your website, it should immediately answer, "Why should I trust this person with my home or business?" If they see your van parked in the neighbourhood, your branding should tell them what you do and why you're the best at it.

Next is the consideration stage. They're weighing up their options – should they call you, or someone else? This is where your reputation comes into play. Your online reviews, testimonials, and case studies matter more than you think. Make it easy for potential clients to see proof of your expertise. Got a video of a job you're especially proud of? Share it. Did a customer leave a review saying you saved the day? Highlight that on your website or social media.

Finally, we've got the decision stage. This is where they pick up the phone, fill out a contact form, or send you a direct message. Don't make them work for it. Your contact details should be everywhere – website, Google My Business, social media profiles – and your response time needs to be quick. Even a short reply like, "Thanks for getting in touch! Let me grab a few details, and we'll book you in," shows you're on top of things.

Removing Friction Points

Nothing kills a potential job faster than unnecessary obstacles. If someone's already stressed about an electrical issue, the last thing they want is to jump through hoops to hire you. Your mission is to remove as much friction as possible from the customer journey.

Start by reviewing your website. Is it easy to navigate? Can someone find your services, pricing (if you display it), and contact information within seconds? If your site looks like it was built in 2005, that's going to turn people off. A clean, modern design with clear headings and buttons can work wonders. And don't forget mobile optimisation – most people are searching for tradespeople on their phones.

Booking a job with you should feel effortless. If you're still relying on back-and-forth emails or missed calls to schedule work, it's time to upgrade. Consider using a scheduling tool that lets clients book appointments directly online. Some systems even send automatic reminders, reducing the chances of no-shows.

Payments are another potential friction point. If you're cash-only or rely on bank transfers, you're putting unnecessary barriers between you and your clients. Offering multiple payment options – card payments, mobile payment apps, even financing for big jobs – shows that you're willing to meet your customers where they're at.

And let's talk about communication. If a customer has to chase you for updates, they're already losing trust. Send them a quick message confirming their appointment, let them know when you're on your way, and follow up afterwards to make sure they're happy with the work. Even if there's a delay or unexpected issue, keeping them in the loop makes a huge difference.

Lastly, think about the physical experience of working with you. Are you turning up in a tidy van and a clean uniform, or does it look like you just rolled out of bed? Are you respectful of their home – laying down dust sheets, cleaning up after yourself, and keeping noise to a minimum? These small details might seem insignificant, but they're the kinds of things customers remember – and talk about.

Tracking Key Metrics Effectively

If you're not tracking your customer journey, you're flying blind. How do you know what's working and what's not? How can you improve if you don't have the data? The good news is, you don't need a fancy software setup or an MBA to start tracking key metrics. A simple system that works for you is all you need.

Start with leads. How many new inquiries are you getting each week or month? Where are they coming from – Google, social media, referrals? If you notice a particular channel is bringing in more business, double down on it. For example, if word-of-mouth referrals are your bread and butter, consider incentivising happy customers to recommend you to others.

Next, track your conversion rate. Of all the people who inquire about your services, how many actually book a job? If that number is low, there might be an issue with your pricing, communication, or the way you're presenting yourself. On the flip side, if your conversion rate is high but you're not getting enough leads, it's time to focus on marketing.

Customer satisfaction is another crucial metric. Are people leaving reviews? What are they saying? If you're not getting feedback, don't be afraid to ask. A quick follow-up message after a job can go a long way: "Thanks for choosing us! If you were happy with our work, we'd really appreciate a review on

Google." And don't just focus on the positives – if someone gives you constructive criticism, use it as an opportunity to improve.

Finally, pay attention to repeat business. How many of your customers come back for additional services? If that number is low, think about how you can stay on their radar – whether it's through email newsletters, seasonal offers, or maintenance reminders.

By tracking these metrics and making adjustments based on the data, you'll not only improve your customer journey but also build a stronger, more profitable business over time.

NETWORKING LIKE A PRO

If you want to grow your business and attract better clients, you can't just rely on your skills as an electrician or tradesperson. You need to tap into the power of relationships. Networking isn't just a buzzword; it's a tool that can open doors to opportunities you didn't even know existed. And no, it's not about handing out business cards like confetti at a wedding. It's about building genuine connections that lead to long-term partnerships and trust. Let's break it down into three actionable areas to make networking work for you.

Building Partnerships with Contractors and Builders

When it comes to partnerships, contractors and builders are your bread and butter. They're the ones who can consistently bring you work and keep your calendar full. But you can't just show up, shake hands, and expect a steady flow of jobs. You've got to bring value to the table.

Start by identifying builders and contractors in your area who align with your work ethic and standards. If they're known for cutting corners or leaving jobs half-done, steer clear. You don't want their reputation rubbing off on yours. Research local projects happening in your area—new housing developments, commercial builds, or even renovations—and find out who's in charge. Then, make your move.

When you reach out, don't just talk about what you do. Focus on how you can make their life easier. Builders and contractors are juggling a million moving parts, and if you can be the reliable, no-drama electrician who delivers on time and on budget, you'll be their go-to. Offer to meet for coffee or swing by their job site to chat. Face-to-face interactions build trust faster than emails or phone calls ever could.

Once you've landed a partnership, treat every job as an audition for the next one. Show up on time, communicate clearly, and don't leave a mess behind. Contractors appreciate tradespeople who make their job easier, and they'll reward you with more work. Don't forget to express your gratitude when they send opportunities your way. A simple thank-you note or a small gesture of appreciation—like a box of biscuits for their team—goes a long way.

Finally, stay in touch even when you're not working on a project together. Send them a quick text to say hello or share a useful tip related to the industry. Relationships need maintenance, just like electrical systems.

Attending Local Events and Trade Shows

Local events and trade shows are goldmines for networking, but only if you approach them strategically. Don't show up aimlessly wandering around and hoping for connections to fall into your lap. Go in with a plan.

Check out the event schedule ahead of time and identify the sessions or exhibitors that are most relevant to your business. If there's a keynote speaker who's an expert in renewable energy or a panel on smart home technology, attend it. Not only will you learn something new, but you'll also have an easy conversation starter when you meet others with shared interests.

When you're at the event, be approachable. Wear a polo shirt with your business logo—something professional but not overly formal. Keep your business cards handy, but don't shove them in people's faces. Instead, focus on having genuine conversations. Ask questions about their work, their challenges, and their goals. People love talking about themselves, and when you show interest, they're more likely to remember you.

It's also worth considering having a small booth at a trade show, especially if you specialise in something unique like EV charger installations or solar panel wiring. A well-designed booth with photos of your work, client testimonials, and maybe even a demo of your services can attract potential clients and collaborators.

After the event, don't let those connections fade away. Follow up within a few days with a quick email or LinkedIn message. Mention something specific from your conversation so they know you were paying attention. Networking is less about who you meet and more about who remembers you—and following up is how you become memorable.

Joining Online Trades Communities

In today's digital age, networking isn't just about handshakes and business cards. There's a whole world of opportunities waiting for you online, and it starts with joining trades-focused communities. These could be Facebook groups, LinkedIn forums, or even niche platforms dedicated to electricians and tradespeople.

Start by finding groups that are active and relevant to your area of expertise. Look for ones where members are sharing tips, asking questions, and genuinely engaging with one another. Avoid groups that are nothing more than spam ads or constant self-promotion. You want to be part of a community that adds value, not noise.

Once you've joined, don't lurk in the shadows. Get involved. Answer questions, share insights, and post updates about your work. If someone's asking for advice on wiring a tricky three-phase circuit or choosing the best tools for a job, chime in with your experience. The more you contribute, the more you'll get noticed as a helpful and knowledgeable professional.

Online communities are also a great place to find collaboration opportunities. For example, you might come across a plumber or HVAC technician who's looking for a reliable electrician to partner with on projects. These alliances can lead to cross-referrals and expand your client base without spending a penny on advertising.

Finally, don't underestimate the power of asking for help. If you're facing a challenge in your business or trying to break into a new market, put it out there. You'll be surprised by how many people are willing to share their advice or connect you with someone who can help. Networking isn't just about what you can get; it's also about what you can give—and the more you give, the more you'll receive in return.

Networking isn't about being pushy or fake. It's about building real relationships with people who can help you grow your business—and who you can help in return. Whether it's forming partnerships with contractors, making connections at local events, or engaging with online communities, the key is to show up, be genuine, and follow through. Electricians who master this skill don't just survive; they thrive.

THE POWER OF CONTENT MARKETING

BLOGGING FOR BUSINESS GROWTH

Let's talk about something that might not be on your radar but absolutely should be: blogging. You might be thinking, "Why does an electrician or trades-person need a blog? Isn't that for tech startups and lifestyle influencers?" Here's the truth: blogging is one of the most effective, low-cost ways to grow your business, establish yourself as an authority, and attract the kind of jobs you actually want to be doing. The best part? It works while you're on the job, asleep, or halfway up a ladder.

Writing How-To Guides for Homeowners

You're sitting on a goldmine of knowledge. Every day, you solve problems that most people don't have the faintest idea how to fix—faulty wiring, flickering lights, tripped circuit breakers. Homeowners are constantly searching for answers to these issues online. That's where you come in.

By writing simple, clear how-to guides, you're not giving away free work; you're positioning yourself as a trusted expert. When you explain, step-by-step, how to check if a circuit breaker has tripped or why an RCD keeps tripping, you're building trust with potential clients. They may read your guide and think, "This sounds straightforward—let me give it a go." But when they realise halfway through that they're in over their heads, who do you think they're going to call? The random name they found on Google, or the expert whose advice they've already read and trusted?

Keep your guides practical and easy to follow. Avoid jargon unless you explain it. For example, don't just say "check the continuity of the circuit." Instead, say, "use a multimeter to check if the electrical current is flowing properly through the circuit. Most multimeters have a continuity setting marked with a sound-wave symbol." This makes you approachable and helpful, not overwhelming.

Pro tip: Always end your guides with a call-to-action (CTA). Something simple like, "If you're not sure or need professional help, give us a ring—we'll sort it for you." This keeps the door open for readers to contact you directly.

Sharing Industry Updates and Trends

The electrical industry is evolving at a faster pace than ever before. From smart home tech to energy-efficient systems, there's always something new happening. Sharing industry updates not only keeps your blog fresh and interesting but also positions you as someone who's on the cutting edge of the trade.

For instance, if there's a new regulation in your area about electrical safety standards or mandatory RCD installations, write about it. Explain what it means for homeowners or businesses and how they can comply without breaking the bank. If a new type of energy-efficient lighting hits the market, talk about the benefits and why it's worth considering.

You don't have to write like a tech journalist. Just keep it conversational. Think of it as if you're explaining it to a mate over a pint. The goal is to make complex topics digestible and show your audience that you're the expert who's already ahead of the curve.

Another angle? Highlight tools or equipment you've started using. Maybe you've switched to a new cable-pulling tool that saves time on jobs or an app that helps you streamline your scheduling. Your audience doesn't just want to know you're skilled—they want to know you're efficient, modern, and reliable.

Using SEO to Drive Traffic

Now, let's get into the nitty-gritty of why blogging works so well: search engine optimisation (SEO). Don't let the term scare you off. It's simpler than it sounds, and it can make a massive difference in how easily people find your business online.

Here's the deal: most people don't scroll past the first page of Google results. If you're not showing up there, you're practically invisible. Blogging helps you climb the rankings by focusing on keywords—those phrases people type into Google when they're looking for help.

For example, if someone searches "how to fix a tripped circuit breaker in Bristol," and you've written a blog post with that exact phrase in the title, guess what? You've just increased your chances of being found.

You don't need to be a tech wizard to get started with SEO. Here are three simple tips to optimise your blog posts: 1. Use specific keywords: Think about the questions your customers ask most often and use those as your blog topics. Include these phrases naturally in your title, headings, and throughout your post. 2. Add meta descriptions: This is the short summary that appears under your blog title in Google search results. Make it clear and enticing. For example: "Learn how to fix a tripped circuit breaker with our easy step-by-step guide. Written by professional electricians in Bristol." 3. Use internal and external links: Link to other pages on your website (like your services page) and also link to credible external sources (like government safety standards). This shows Google that your content is both helpful and trustworthy.

Don't forget to include images or videos in your blog posts. A photo of a neatly wired fuse box or a quick video explaining the difference between single-phase and three-phase power can make your posts even more engaging. Just make sure to add "Alt text" to your images—this is another chance to include your keywords and help Google understand what your page is about.

Finally, consistency is key. You don't need to blog every week, but aim for at least one post a month. Over time, this builds up a library of helpful content that keeps driving traffic to your website. It's like planting seeds that grow into a forest of opportunities.

Your blog isn't just a page on your website—it's a magnet for potential clients. Use it to share your knowledge, showcase your expertise, and let people know you're the electrician or trades-person they've been looking for.

VIDEO MARKETING MADE SIMPLE

You've probably heard it before: Video is king. And for good reason. It's the most engaging, digestible, and shareable form of content on the internet right now. Whether you're rewiring a home, installing a new smart system, or troubleshooting a faulty circuit, video allows you to showcase your expertise in a way that words and images simply can't. But let's get one thing straight—you don't need a Hollywood budget or a professional film crew to make video marketing work for you. All you need is a smartphone, a few good ideas, and a bit of consistency. Let's break it down.

Showcasing Your Work with Before-and-After Clips

People love a good transformation story, and as an electrician or trades-person, you've got these stories happening daily. Whether you're installing sleek new downlights in a dated kitchen or tidying up a jungle of wires in a dodgy old breaker box, the contrast between "before" and "after" is your secret weapon.

Start by capturing the "before" shot. Show the mess, the chaos, or the outdated setup. Don't be afraid to narrate what's wrong or why it needs fixing. For instance, say something like, "This is the old consumer unit—completely outdated and doesn't meet today's safety standards. We're going to replace it with a modern RCBO board that's safer and more efficient."

Once the work is done, record the "after" shot. Show the clean, professional finish and explain the benefits. Maybe it's safer, more energy-efficient, or simply better looking. Keep the tone confident but not overly technical—your goal is to educate, not confuse. A quick comparison between the two clips stitched together with some simple editing software (CapCut or InShot are great free options) can work wonders.

The key is to keep it real. Don't overthink the production quality. People relate to authenticity, not perfection. A shaky handheld shot and a genuine explanation will often resonate more than a polished, scripted video. If you're proud of the work, it will show, and that's what your audience cares about.

Creating Quick Tips Videos

You'd be surprised how much trust you can build by giving away a little free advice. Think about the questions you get asked all the time: "Why does my light flicker?" "How can I reset my circuit breaker?" "What's the difference between halogen and LED bulbs?" These common queries are goldmines for content.

Pick one question, hit record, and explain the answer in under two minutes. Keep it simple—pretend you're explaining it to your mate down the pub. For example, if you're talking about flickering lights, you might say, "If your light flickers, it could just be a loose bulb. Turn it off, tighten it, and see if that helps. If not, it might be an issue with the wiring—something I'd recommend getting checked out by a professional." Boom, you've provided value in under 30 seconds.

Short tips like these are perfect for platforms like Instagram Reels, TikTok, or YouTube Shorts. They're quick to make, easy for people to digest, and great for building familiarity with your brand. The more helpful you are, the more likely people are to remember you when they need a professional.

You can even tie your tips to seasonal themes for extra relevance. For example, in the colder months, you could create a video about how to check if your home is winter-ready electrically. Or during summer, you might share tips on setting up outdoor lighting for barbecues and garden parties.

Hosting Live Q&A Sessions

There's something powerful about showing up live. It's unfiltered, unscripted, and raw—and that's exactly why people love it. Hosting a live Q&A session on Facebook, Instagram, or even LinkedIn can position you as the trusted expert people turn to.

The idea is simple: Announce in advance that you'll be going live to answer electrical questions. Promote it on your social media channels and encourage your followers to submit questions ahead of time. When it's time to go live, make sure you're in a quiet, well-lit space (your van parked in a quiet spot works perfectly!). Start by introducing yourself and what you do, then dive into the questions.

Don't worry if no one asks anything at first—have a few commonly asked questions prepared to get the ball rolling. For instance, "One thing I get asked a lot is, 'Do I really need an RCD in my home?' The answer is 100% yes—it's a safety device that can save lives by cutting off the power in dangerous situations."

As people start engaging, keep the tone conversational and

approachable. Don't be afraid to crack a joke or share a quick story about a memorable job (as long as it respects client privacy, of course). The more personable you are, the more people will connect with you.

Live sessions are also a great opportunity to plug your services subtly. For example, if someone asks about upgrading their wiring, you can say, "That's definitely something I can help with. Feel free to DM me after this, and we'll sort it out." It's not pushy—it's helpful.

And here's the beauty of live content: Once the session is done, you can save it and repurpose it as a regular video. Trim out any awkward pauses or tech hiccups, and you've got another piece of content for your library.

Video marketing doesn't have to be complicated or time-consuming—it just requires you to show up, share your expertise, and let your personality shine through. Whether it's a polished before-and-after showcase, a quick tip on fixing a common problem, or a live Q&A session, video can help you build trust, increase visibility, and ultimately attract more clients who already see you as the go-to expert.

EMAIL MARKETING THAT WORKS

Let's face it—email often gets a bad rap. It's easy to dismiss it as outdated in a world dominated by social media and instant messaging. But here's the thing: email is still one of the most powerful, cost-effective tools you have for staying connected with your clients and keeping your business top of mind. You're not just sending messages; you're building relationships, driving repeat business, and creating opportunities to up-sell your services. The best part? Unlike social media algorithms that decide who sees your posts, email goes directly into your customer's inbox. It's a direct line to your audience, and it's yours to own.

So, let's break it down into three actionable strategies: crafting engaging newsletters, offering special deals and updates, and automating follow-ups.

Crafting Engaging Newsletters

Think of your newsletter as a conversation starter, not a sales pitch. People don't open emails to be bombarded with ads; they open them because they're curious, they trust you, and they think you might have something useful to share. So, what can you offer that's worth their time?

Start with valuable content. You're in the trades, so you're sitting on a goldmine of practical knowledge. Share quick tips that homeowners can use to maintain their electrical systems safely. For instance, talk about how to test smoke alarms or the importance of upgrading old fuse boxes. Keep it simple, actionable, and jargon-free. You're not trying to teach them how to rewire their house; you're positioning yourself as the expert they'll call when they need help.

Then, add a personal touch. Share a story from the field—maybe you solved a tricky problem for a customer or completed a unique project you're proud of. This isn't just about showing off your skills; it's about humanising your brand. People hire people, not faceless businesses, so let them see the person behind the tools.

Don't forget to include visuals. A photo of your latest project or a short video walk-through of a job can make your email pop. You don't need a professional photographer; a well-lit shot from your smartphone will do the trick. Just make sure it's clear and not cluttered with distractions.

Finally, keep your emails short and to the point. Your readers are busy, just like you. They don't have time to wade through walls of text. Use bullet points, break up paragraphs, and make it easy to skim. And whatever you do, make sure there's a clear call-to-action (CTA). Whether it's "Book a free consultation" or "Visit our website for more tips," tell them exactly what you want them to do next.

Offering Special Deals and Updates

Everyone loves a good deal. Offering special promotions in your emails is a sure-fire way to grab attention and drive action. But this isn't about slashing your prices to the bone; it's about creating offers that add value while showcasing your expertise.

Start with seasonal campaigns. Think about the times of

year when your customers are likely to need your services the most. Summer might be perfect for promoting air conditioning installations or garden lighting setups. Winter could be all about electrical inspections to ensure homes are safe and cosy for the holidays. Frame your offers around solving a specific problem or making their lives easier.

Loyalty discounts are another great way to keep your existing customers coming back. Maybe it's 10% off for repeat clients or a free safety check for customers who've used your services within the past year. These kinds of offers not only show appreciation but also encourage long-term relationships.

Exclusive updates can also set you apart. Let your email subscribers be the first to know about new services, equipment upgrades, or certifications you've earned. For example, if you've just started offering smart home installations, send out an email explaining the benefits and why you're the electrician for the job. This not only keeps your audience informed but also positions you as a forward-thinking professional.

Don't underestimate the power of urgency. Phrases like "Offer ends this Friday" or "Limited slots available" can push people to take action now rather than later. Just make sure you follow through and genuinely limit the availability—false urgency can backfire and damage your credibility.

Finally, track what works. Use email marketing software to see which offers get the most clicks and conversions. This data will help you refine your strategy and focus on what your audience responds to best.

Automating Follow-Ups to Stay Connected

Here's where you save time and stay consistent without lifting a finger: automation. Setting up automated email sequences is like having a virtual assistant that works 24/7, keeping your clients engaged even when you're busy on a job.

Start with a welcome email. When someone signs up for your newsletter, books a service, or requests a quote, send them an automated message thanking them for getting in touch. This isn't just polite; it sets the tone for your relationship. Use this opportunity to introduce yourself, share a bit about your business, and let them know what they can expect from you.

Next, think about post-job follow-ups. A week after completing a job, send an email asking how everything's going. Encourage them to reply if they have any questions or concerns. This shows you care about their satisfaction and aren't just moving on to the next client. It's also a great time to ask for a review. Make it easy by including a direct link to your preferred review platform.

Seasonal reminders are another powerful tool. Set up emails to go out at key times of year with maintenance tips or service offers. For example, in the autumn, you could send a message about preparing electrical systems for winter storms, along with an offer for a discounted inspection. These reminders keep you relevant and top of mind without feeling intrusive.

Finally, don't forget about re-engagement emails. If a customer hasn't booked your services in a while, send them a friendly nudge. Maybe it's a special offer or a reminder about the last job you did for them. Keep it light and helpful, not pushy. Sometimes all it takes is a little prompt to bring them back.

Automation doesn't mean you're losing the personal touch. You can still customise your emails with the recipient's name or reference their previous interactions with you. The goal is to stay connected in a way that feels natural and effortless—for both you and your clients.

With these strategies, email marketing becomes more than just another item on your to-do list; it transforms into a reliable workhorse for your business. You'll not only keep your existing customers engaged but also open the door to new opportunities—all while focusing on what you do best: delivering exceptional service.

WINNING AT CUSTOMER RETENTION

THE ART OF EXCEPTIONAL CUSTOMER SERVICE

Let's get straight to it: your ability to deliver outstanding customer service can make or break your business. In the trades industry, where trust and reliability are everything, exceptional service isn't just a nice-to-have—it's your secret weapon. You're not just wiring homes or fixing circuits; you're building relationships, one satisfied customer at a time.

If you think customer service is simply about showing up on time and doing a decent job, you're playing small. The tradespeople who dominate their markets understand that service is an experience. Every interaction—whether it's a phone call, a job site visit, or a follow-up email—is an opportunity to leave a lasting impression. When you nail this, you'll not only keep your customers coming back, but you'll also turn them into your biggest advocates.

Communicating Clearly and Professionally

Let's start with communication. If your customers aren't clear about what's happening, they'll fill the gaps with assumptions—and not the good kind. You've probably heard horror stories about tradespeople who don't return calls, show up late with no explanation, or leave clients wondering what they're paying for. Don't be that person.

When you first engage with a client, set the tone by being professional yet approachable. Answer your phone or return calls promptly. Speak in plain language—nobody wants to hear you rattle off jargon about three-phase motors or IP ratings they don't understand. Break it down in a way that makes sense to them.

For example, if you're quoting for a job, be crystal clear about what's included and what isn't. A simple phrase like, "This price covers the installation of sockets and switches, but rewiring additional circuits would be extra," can save you from awkward conversations down the line. Transparency builds trust.

When you're on site, keep the customer in the loop. Before you start, walk them through what you're planning to do. If something unexpected comes up—like discovering dodgy old wiring that needs replacing—stop and explain the situation before proceeding. This shows that you respect their home and their wallet.

Finally, always follow up. Once the job's done, send a quick text or email thanking them for their business and confirming everything's working as it should be. It's a small gesture that makes a big difference.

Going the Extra Mile with Small Gestures

Here's the thing: customers expect you to do a good job. That's the baseline. What sets you apart is the little things that show you care. These don't have to cost much, but they leave a lasting impression.

Let's say you've just finished installing a new fuse board. Before you pack up, take a few minutes to tidy up the area—not just your tools, but the dust and debris too. Sure, it's not technically your responsibility, but a clean workspace speaks volumes about your professionalism.

Or maybe you're replacing outdoor lighting for a homeowner. Once the job's done, offer to adjust their security camera angle to align with the new setup. It's a two-minute task for you but might save them a world of hassle.

Even something as simple as wearing clean shoe covers inside a customer's home can make a big difference. It shows respect for their property and reassures them they've made the right choice hiring you.

Another powerful gesture is remembering your customers. Imagine the impact of saying something like, "How's the extension coming along that you were telling me about last time?" It's not hard to keep a few notes on your phone about repeat clients, and it makes them feel valued.

And don't underestimate the power of a handwritten thank-you note. Yes, it's old-school, but that's precisely why it works. After finishing a big project, pop a card in the post thanking the client for trusting you with their home. It's an unexpected touch that keeps you top of mind.

Handling Complaints Gracefully

Let's be real—no matter how good you are, things will occasionally go wrong. A part doesn't work as expected, a deadline gets missed, or a customer misinterprets what was agreed. How you handle these moments can define your reputation.

The first rule of handling complaints is simple: don't get defensive. Your initial reaction might be to explain why it's not your fault, but resist the urge. Instead, listen. Let the customer vent if they need to, and acknowledge their feelings. Phrases like, "I can see why you're frustrated," or "I understand where you're coming from," go a long way in diffusing tension.

Next, take ownership. Even if the issue wasn't directly your fault, it's your responsibility to make it right. Saying, "Let me look into this and get it sorted for you," shows that you're proactive and solutions-focused.

Once you've identified the problem, fix it quickly and efficiently. If it's a straightforward issue—like replacing a faulty light fitting—schedule the repair as soon as possible. If it's more complex, keep the customer updated on your progress. Silence is your enemy here; even a quick message saying, "Just to let you know, I've ordered the replacement part and it should arrive tomorrow," keeps them in the loop and reassures them you're on it.

Finally, learn from the experience. Was there a miscommunication that could have been avoided? Could you tweak your processes to prevent similar issues in the future? Every complaint is an opportunity to improve.

Remember, customers don't expect perfection—they expect accountability. Handling complaints with grace can turn a disgruntled client into a loyal one. As the saying goes, "It's not the mistake that matters; it's how you fix it."

—- Customer service isn't just a box to tick—it's the foundation of a thriving business. The tradespeople who truly succeed are the ones who treat every customer as if they're their most important client. When you focus on clear communication, thoughtful gestures, and handling issues with professionalism, you're not just delivering a service—you're building a reputation that lasts.

BUILDING LOYALTY PROGRAMMES

When it comes to customer loyalty, you're playing the long game. A loyalty programme isn't just a nice-to-have feature; it's a powerful tool that keeps your best customers coming back while turning them into your most vocal advocates. Think of it as building a community around your business—one where your clients feel appreciated, valued, and rewarded for sticking with you. Let's break it down into three actionable parts.

Incentivising Repeat Business

Loyalty is driven by consistency. When customers know they'll get excellent service every time, they're more likely to call you back. But what if you sweeten the deal? Small perks and incentives can make a massive difference in how often your clients choose you over someone else.

Start with something simple. Offer a "5th Job Free" punch card system for smaller services like safety inspections or quick fixes. If you're in the habit of doing annual electrical checks for homeowners, offer a discount for repeat bookings. For example, their second inspection could be 10% off, and their third one 20% off. Over time, they'll see the value in sticking with you rather than shopping around.

Don't underestimate the power of bundling. Instead of just offering one-off services, create packages for ongoing maintenance. For example, you could offer a yearly subscription that includes two routine inspections, priority scheduling, and discounted rates on emergency call-outs. This not only secures repeat business but also provides predictable cash flow for you.

Make it personal. If you know a customer has just had a big rewiring job done, offer them a discounted surge protector installation as a follow-up. Tailored suggestions show that you're not just trying to sell them something—they'll feel like you genuinely care about their safety and satisfaction.

Lastly, keep it simple. A complicated loyalty programme with endless rules and exceptions is a quick way to lose interest. Your customers are busy, just like you. Make sure the process to earn and redeem rewards is as easy as flipping a light switch.

Offering Exclusive Member Perks

Everyone loves to feel like they're part of an exclusive club, and your business can provide that. Offering perks to loyal customers builds a sense of belonging and gives people something special to talk about.

Start by creating a VIP list. This doesn't have to be overly formal—just a simple system where your most loyal customers get early access to deals, priority time slots, or even free upgrades. For example, if you're running a special on EV charger installations or smart home upgrades, let your VIPs know first. Drop them an email or give them a quick call. They'll appreciate the personal touch and the chance to grab the offer before it's advertised publicly.

Think beyond discounts. Sometimes, exclusive perks can be about convenience or priority. For instance, offer your loyal customers a guaranteed 24-hour response time for emergencies, even during peak periods. This kind of assurance is invaluable to someone who relies on your services, and it costs you nothing but smart scheduling.

Another angle? Partner with local businesses to create joint perks. If you know a plumber, roofer, or even a local coffee shop owner, arrange a cross-promotion. For example, your VIP customers could get a discount at the coffee shop, while their loyal patrons get a discount on your electrical services. It's a win-win for everyone involved, and it strengthens your ties to the local community too.

Finally, don't forget about the power of small, unexpected gestures. A handwritten thank-you card after a big job, a free upgrade on a service, or even something as simple as a branded magnet or keyring can leave a lasting impression. It's not the monetary value that matters—it's the thought behind it.

Tracking and Rewarding Referrals

Your best customers are also your best advocates. When someone recommends your services to their friends or family, it's because they trust you'll deliver the same quality they've come to expect. So why not reward them for spreading the word?

Set up a referral system that's clear and enticing. For example, for every new client someone refers to you, they could receive a £50 credit towards their next service or a gift card to a local business. Make sure the reward is significant enough to motivate action but not so extravagant that it eats into your profits.

Be transparent about how the system works. Let your clients know they don't need to do anything complicated—just share your name and number with their contacts. You can even provide them with pre-designed referral cards or a digital link they can share via text or email.

Take it a step further by making the referral process feel like a mutually beneficial exchange. For instance, offer something to the new customer as well, like a 10% discount on their first job. This creates goodwill right from the start and makes it easier for your loyal clients to recommend you without hesitation.

Don't forget to track referrals properly. Whether you're using software or an old-school spreadsheet, make sure every referral is logged and rewarded promptly. Nothing kills goodwill faster than a delayed or forgotten reward.

And don't stop at individual referrals. If you have a strong relationship with a contractor, builder, or property manager who frequently sends work your way, consider rewarding them on a larger scale. This could be through quarterly bonuses, exclusive discounts, or even co-branded marketing efforts that benefit both parties.

Remember to shout about your referral programme. Include it in your email signature, mention it in your newsletters, and bring it up during conversations with happy customers. Most people won't think to refer you unless you plant the seed.

Lastly, celebrate your advocates. Highlight your top referrers in a newsletter or on social media (with their permission, of course). Something as simple as "A big thank you to John Smith for referring three new clients this month!" can go a long way in keeping the momentum going. Plus, it subtly reminds others to get involved too.

When you build loyalty programmes that incentivise repeat business, offer exclusive perks, and reward referrals effectively, you're not just creating satisfied customers—you're building raving fans who will champion your business for years to come.

STAYING IN TOUCH POST-JOB

You've wrapped up the job, the client's happy, and you're off to the next site. Job done, right? Not quite. The work you've just completed is only part of the equation—what you do after the job can be the difference between a one-off customer and a loyal client for life. Staying in touch post-job isn't about pestering people or hard-selling them on services they don't need; it's about maintaining a relationship, staying top of mind, and ensuring they think of you first when they—or someone they know—needs an electrician.

Sending Follow-Up Messages

Think about this: how often do customers remember to leave a glowing review or recommend you to a friend without a nudge? Not often. A simple follow-up message can work wonders. The day after the job is complete, send them a quick, professional text or email. Something like:

"Hi [Name], just wanted to check in and make sure everything is working perfectly after the job yesterday. If you have any questions or concerns, feel free to reach out! Also, if you're happy with the work, it would mean a lot if you could leave us a review on [Google/Facebook/etc.]. Thanks again for choosing [Your Business Name]!"

This isn't just about reviews—it's about showing you care. You're not just a trades-person; you're someone who's genuinely invested in the satisfaction of your clients. If something's not right, this gives them a chance to tell you directly, rather than letting frustration fester or airing grievances online.

For bigger jobs, consider following up again a few weeks later. Ask if everything's still running smoothly. This kind of attention to detail sets you apart and builds trust. It shows you're not just there to collect payment and vanish.

Offering Seasonal Maintenance Reminders

Electricity is one of those things people don't think about until something goes wrong. That's where you come in. Seasonal maintenance reminders are an easy way to stay in touch while providing value. For example, as winter approaches, send out an email or social media post reminding clients to check their outdoor lighting or ensure their heating systems are in top shape. Something like:

"Winter is coming—make sure your electrical systems are ready! Outdoor lighting, heating circuits, and safety checks are crucial this time of year. Give us a call if you'd like us to take a look."

Or, in the spring:

"Spring clean your home's electrical system! It's the perfect time to test your smoke alarms, check outdoor wiring, and make sure everything's running efficiently."

These reminders position you as a proactive problem solver, not just someone they call in an emergency. You're showing them you care about their long-term safety and convenience. And while some people might not take action right away, you'll be the one they think of when they do.

If you're using a customer database, set up reminders for specific clients based on the work you've done. Installed a new fuse board? Set a reminder to check in a year later to ensure everything's still in order. Rewired a home? Suggest a periodic inspection to keep things safe. These customised touches show you're paying attention, not just churning out jobs.

Staying Active on Social Media

Social media might not be the first thing that comes to mind when you think about staying in touch, but it's a low-effort, high-impact way to keep your business in front of your clients. The trick is to post content that's useful, engaging, and relevant—not just "Here's another job we've done" every week.

Think about the common questions or issues your clients face. Are they wondering how to reset a tripped breaker? Unsure why their energy bills are so high? Create short posts or videos addressing these topics. For example:

- A 30-second video: "Here's how to safely reset your breaker if it trips. Remember—if it keeps happening, give us a call to investigate what's going on." - A quick post: "Did you know LED lights use up to 75% less energy than traditional bulbs? A simple switch could save you money every month."

You don't need to overcomplicate it—just focus on adding value. When people see you sharing helpful advice, you're not just an electrician; you're someone they trust to know their stuff.

Don't underestimate the power of before-and-after photos,

either. A photo of a messy fuse box next to a neatly rewired one speaks volumes about your professionalism. Tag the location (with the client's permission, of course) and caption it with something like: "Another home made safer with a fuse board upgrade. If your system's more than 10 years old, it might be time for a check-up!"

Beyond posting, make sure you're engaging with your audience. Reply to comments, answer questions, and thank people for their kind words. It's not about spending hours online—it's about showing that you're approachable and attentive.

Social media is also a great place to share updates about your business. Are you introducing new services? Offering a limited-time discount? Supporting a local event? Keep your followers in the loop. Even if they don't need your services right now, they'll remember you when they do.

And don't forget about local community groups on Facebook or Next-door. These are goldmines for tradespeople. Someone's always asking, "Does anyone know a good electrician?" Jump into the comments with a friendly reply, sharing your contact details and a link to your website or Google reviews. Be helpful and professional—the goal is to build trust, not spam people.

When you stay in touch post-job, you're not just building a customer base—you're creating a network of loyal clients who will sing your praises to their friends, family, and neighbours. It's not about being pushy; it's about being present. Whether it's a quick follow-up message, a seasonal reminder, or a helpful post on social media, every interaction reinforces your reputation as the go-to expert. And in a business where trust is everything, that's how you become unforgettable.

SCALING WITHOUT LOSING YOUR TOUCH

HIRING AND TRAINING YOUR TEAM

As a sparky who's built something you're proud of, there comes a time when scaling up isn't just an option—it's a necessity. The phone rings more than you can answer, jobs are stacking up, and you're starting to think, "I can't do this all on my own anymore." That's a good problem to have, but it's also when things can go sideways fast if you bring the wrong people on board. Hiring and training your team isn't just about filling gaps; it's about building a crew that carries your brand, your reputation, and your standards into every job they tackle.

Identifying the Right Candidates

Hiring the right people starts with knowing exactly what you're looking for. You're not just hiring someone to run conduit or wire up a new build; you're bringing someone into your brand's ecosystem. The first thing to ask yourself is: what qualities matter most?

Technical skills are a given. If someone can't strip wire without nicking it or doesn't know the difference between a single-phase and three-phase system, they're not for you. But skills can be taught; attitude is harder to mould. You want people who show up on time, communicate clearly, and genuinely care about doing a job right. Look for a mix of humility and hunger—someone who wants to learn but is also confident enough to tackle problems head-on.

Here's the thing: experience can be a double-edged sword. Sure, a seasoned electrician might seem like a no-brainer, but if they're stuck in their ways or unwilling to adapt to how you do things, they could be more trouble than they're worth. Sometimes, hiring a green apprentice with the right mindset and work ethic is a better investment than hiring a "know-it-all" who resists training.

Where do you find the right candidates? First, ask your network. Talk to suppliers, other tradespeople, or even clients who might know someone looking for a role in the industry. Job boards are fine, but referrals tend to bring in people who are already vouched for. And when you put out the job ad, be clear about what you stand for. Mention your commitment to quality, customer service, and teamwork. It'll help filter out those who don't align with your vision.

Finally, during interviews, don't just ask about technical stuff. Ask how they'd handle an angry client, what they'd do if they made a mistake on the job, or how they'd prioritise tasks when under pressure. Their answers will tell you a lot about whether they'll fit into your operation.

Onboarding with a Focus on Your Brand

The first few weeks with a new hire are critical. This isn't just about showing them where the coffee machine is or handing them a uniform. It's about indoctrinating them into your way of doing things.

Start by giving them the lay of the land. Walk them through your company's history, your values, and your vision for the future. Share your brand story—the one you crafted in Chapter 1. Tell them why you started this business, the kind of clients you serve, and what sets you apart from the competition. This isn't fluff; it's how you get buy-in from your team. When they understand your "why," they'll take more pride in being part of it.

Next, set crystal-clear expectations. What does "a job well done" look like to you? How should they handle customer interactions? What's the protocol if something unexpected comes up on-site? Don't assume they'll pick it up as they go. Document your standards and processes in a simple, no-nonsense manual or guidebook. If you're not the type to write things down, record a series of short videos explaining how you like things done.

Here's a pro-level move: pair new hires with a seasoned team member who embodies your values. This isn't just about showing them how to run cable or install a fuse board; it's about demonstrating how to interact with clients, clean up after a job, and represent your brand with professionalism.

And don't forget the feedback loop. Check in regularly during their first few weeks—daily, if needed. Ask what they're finding challenging, where they feel confident, and what they think could be improved. This isn't about micromanaging; it's about setting them up for success while showing them you care about their development.

Training for Consistent Customer Experience

When you think about training, don't limit it to technical skills. Sure, your crew needs to know their way around a multimeter and understand the latest wiring regulations, but that's table stakes. What sets your business apart is the experience you deliver to customers—and that's where training should take centre stage.

Start with communication. Teach your team how to greet clients, explain complex issues in plain English, and keep them updated throughout the job. Customers don't want to feel left in the dark—literally or figuratively. Role-play scenarios with your team. For example, how should they handle a client who's upset because the job is taking longer than expected? What's the best way to explain a change order without making it sound like you're just trying to up-sell them? These aren't soft skills; they're survival skills in this industry.

Next, focus on the details that customers notice but rarely mention. Things like wearing branded uniforms, parking the van neatly, and cleaning up thoroughly after the job. Yes, it's basic, but these are the things that get you referrals and glowing reviews. Make sure your team knows that a tidy workspace and a polite demeanour are just as important as getting the wiring right.

Finally, keep training ongoing. The electrical industry doesn't stand still, and neither should your team's knowledge. Set aside time for regular training sessions, whether it's brushing up on changes to the Wiring Regulations or learning about emerging technologies like EV chargers or smart home systems. Bring in experts if you need to. The more your team knows, the more valuable they'll be—not just to you, but to your clients.

And don't underestimate the power of cross-training. If one of your team members is a up-sell at fault finding but struggles with customer service, pair them with someone who excels in that area so they can learn from each other. The goal is to create a team that's not just skilled but well-rounded.

Scaling your business doesn't mean diluting your standards. It means replicating them across every member of your team, every interaction with a client, and every job you take on. Get your hiring, onboarding, and training right, and you'll not only grow—you'll thrive.

STREAMLINING YOUR OPERATIONS

Running a tight ship is the difference between surviving and thriving in the trades industry. The more you can streamline your operations, the more time you'll have to focus on the work that matters—delivering exceptional service to your customers and growing your business. Efficiency isn't about cutting corners; it's about cutting out waste—wasted time, wasted energy, and wasted resources. Let's dig into how you can streamline your operations so your business runs like a finely tuned machine.

Using Scheduling Software

Time is money, especially in the trades. If you're still juggling a paper diary or relying on a whiteboard in your garage to keep track of jobs, it's time to upgrade. Scheduling software isn't just some fancy tech for big corporations; it's a game-changer for small businesses.

The right scheduling tool helps you manage your jobs, team, and resources all in one place. No more double-booking a job or losing track of where your team is supposed to be. You can assign tasks, set deadlines, and even send reminders to your team directly from the app. Many platforms also let you sync schedules with your team's smartphones, so everyone's on the same page without needing daily phone calls to confirm details.

Look for software that integrates with other tools you're already using. For instance, if you issue invoices via QuickBooks, find scheduling software that works seamlessly with it. If you're using Google Calendar, make sure your scheduling tool can sync with it. The smoother the transition, the more likely you'll use it consistently.

Don't overcomplicate things. You don't need a flashy system with a hundred features you'll never use. Start with something lean that handles the basics—job scheduling, time tracking, and reminders. Many tools are designed specifically for tradespeople, so they're built with your needs in mind. Options like Tradify, Fergus, or ServiceM8 are worth exploring.

Once you've got your scheduling software up and running, take the time to input all your recurring jobs and maintenance contracts. This ensures nothing slips through the cracks. You'll also want to build in buffers for unexpected delays. Jobs in the trades rarely go 100% to plan, so don't stack your schedule so tight that a small hiccup throws the whole day off.

Managing Inventory Efficiently

How many times have you turned up to a job, only to realise you're missing something essential? It's frustrating, unprofessional, and costs you money. Managing your inventory doesn't need to be a full-time job, but it does need to be intentional.

Start by organising what you've got. If your work van looks

more like a dumping ground than a professionals mobile office, it's time for a clear-out. Categorise your stock: cables, fittings, tools, testing equipment—all of it. Use labelled bins or storage boxes to keep everything in its place. The goal is to make it as easy as possible to find what you need without rummaging.

Once your workspace is organised, you need a system to track what you've got and what you're running low on. An inventory management app can help with this. Options like Sortly or Trade Trak let you log your stock levels and even set alerts for when you're running low on specific items. If you're not ready to go digital, a simple spreadsheet can work as long as you update it regularly.

The key to efficient inventory management is staying proactive. Create a habit of checking stock levels weekly or bi-weekly. When you're restocking, don't just think about what you need now; consider what you'll likely need for upcoming jobs. It's always better to have a little extra on hand than to be caught short.

Bulk buying can also save you money and time. If you know certain materials—like conduit, sockets, or cable ties—are staples in your work, buy them in larger quantities. Just make sure you've got the storage space to keep them organised. And don't forget to keep an eye on expiry dates for things like adhesives or insulation materials.

Finally, make it easy for your team to grab what they need without turning your van or workshop into a free-for-all. Implement a simple check-out system so you know who's taken what and when. This not only keeps everyone accountable but also helps you track usage trends over time.

Creating Standard Operating Procedures (SOPs)

Consistency is king when it comes to delivering top-notch service and running an efficient business. Standard Operating Procedures (SOPs) are the playbook for how you and your team handle every aspect of your work, from quoting jobs to following up with customers.

Think of SOPs as your business's cheat sheet. They take the guesswork out of day-to-day operations and ensure everyone on your team knows exactly what's expected of them. Start by identifying the key processes in your business. This could include: - Taking customer enquiries - Conducting site inspections - Preparing quotes - Ordering materials - Completing installations or repairs - Issuing invoices - Following up on payments

For each process, break it down into step-by-step instructions. Keep it simple and straightforward—this isn't the time for jargon or overly technical language. The goal is to create a guide that anyone on your team could follow, even if they're new to the job.

Once you've documented your SOPs, get your team involved. Ask for their input and feedback, especially for tasks they handle regularly. They might spot gaps or suggest improvements that you hadn't considered. The more buy-in you get from your team, the more likely they'll follow the procedures consistently.

SOPs aren't set in stone. They should evolve as your business grows and as you find better ways to do things. Schedule regular reviews—maybe once a quarter or twice a year—to make sure they're still relevant and effective.

Beyond improving efficiency, SOPs are a critical tool for training new hires. Instead of spending hours walking someone through every little detail, you can hand them the playbook and let them get up to speed on their own. This frees you up to focus on higher-level tasks that drive your business forward.

To make your SOPs even more impactful, consider creating video tutorials for complex tasks. A quick video showing how to use specific software, tools, or equipment can save hours of back-and-forth explanations. Store these videos in a shared drive or team portal so they're easily accessible.

When you've got clear SOPs in place, you're not just streamlining operations; you're protecting your brand. Every customer interaction becomes a reflection of your professionalism and attention to detail. And in a competitive market, that's what sets you apart.

By investing time and energy into these three areas—scheduling software, inventory management, and SOPs—you'll create a business that operates smoothly and efficiently. You'll reduce stress, cut out unnecessary headaches, and free up more time to focus on what really matters: delivering exceptional service and growing your business.

MAINTAINING QUALITY CONTROL

Conducting Regular Job Inspections

You know the saying, "What gets measured gets managed"? It's not just corporate jargon—it's a golden rule for any tradesperson who wants to deliver top-notch work, every time. Job inspections aren't about nitpicking or playing the blame game. They're about ensuring your team delivers work that aligns with your standards, because at the end of the day, your name is on the line.

Start by making inspections a habit, not an afterthought. Whether you're running a one-man operation or managing a growing team, carve out time to review completed jobs. It doesn't have to be an elaborate process. A quick site visit to check the quality of work, the cleanliness of the area, and adherence to safety standards can make a world of difference. You're not just looking at the technical execution of the job—though that's obviously critical—you're also assessing the overall customer experience.

Create a simple checklist tailored to your trade. Think about the key things your clients care about: Is the wiring neat and tidy? Are the fixtures aligned properly? Was everything cleaned up afterwards? A checklist keeps you focused and ensures consistency across projects. It also gives you a framework to provide constructive feedback to your team, rather than vague criticisms that leave them guessing.

Don't just inspect the big jobs. Smaller projects, like a socket repair or installing a light fitting, deserve the same attention. Why? Because every job is an opportunity to reinforce your reputation. If a customer sees you care about the details, they're more likely to trust you with bigger, more complex work in the future.

And here's something to keep in mind: inspections shouldn't be a solo gig. If you've got a team, involve them in the process. Make it collaborative. Walk through the site together, point out what went well, and discuss areas for improvement. It's not about barking orders—it's about creating a culture of pride in the quality of your work.

Collecting Customer Feedback

If you really want to know how you're doing, ask the people who matter most: your customers. Customer feedback is like gold dust—it gives you an unfiltered view of what's working and what isn't. But here's the thing: if you don't make it easy for customers to share their thoughts, most of them won't bother. They're busy, just like you.

Start by asking for feedback immediately after a job is completed. You're more likely to get honest, useful responses when the experience is still fresh in their minds. A quick follow-up call or email can work wonders. Keep it simple. Ask two or three specific questions, like "Were you happy with the quality of work?" or "Was our team professional and courteous?" Don't overwhelm them with a 10-minute survey—they'll tune out.

For those customers who seem particularly happy with your work, take the opportunity to dig a little deeper. Ask them what stood out about your service or what made them choose you over a competitor. These insights can help you refine your processes and highlight your strengths in future marketing efforts.

Not all feedback will be glowing, and that's a good thing. Constructive criticism is your chance to improve. If a customer flags something they weren't happy with, take it seriously. Acknowledge their concerns, thank them for their honesty, and assure them that you'll address the issue. Then follow through. Nothing builds trust like showing you're willing to learn and adapt.

You can also use feedback as a training tool for your team. Share customer comments—both positive and negative—in your next team meeting. Celebrate the wins, and use the criticisms as teachable moments. When your team sees that you value feedback and act on it, they'll be more motivated to strive for excellence.

Improving Processes Based on Insights

Feedback and inspections are only as valuable as the action you take from them. If you're not using what you learn to tweak and improve your processes, you're leaving money on the table. Think of every bit of insight—whether it comes from a customer, a team member, or your own observations—as a stepping stone to a better business.

Start by looking for patterns. If multiple customers mention that your team left behind a mess, it's not just an isolated issue—it's a process problem. Maybe your clean-up protocol needs revisiting, or maybe it's time to invest in better tools for tidying up quickly. The same goes for positive feedback. If customers keep raving about how friendly and professional your team is, lean into that. Make customer service training a bigger focus during onboarding.

Technology can be your best ally here. Use a simple project management tool or even just a shared spreadsheet to track issues and improvements. If a team member suggests a better way to install a certain type of fixture, document it. If a customer loves the way you explained their new smart home system, make that part of your standard handover process. Over time, these small changes add up to big improvements.

Don't forget to communicate these changes to your team. If you've implemented a new protocol based on feedback, explain why it matters. People are more likely to embrace change when they understand the "why" behind it. Plus, involving your team in the process shows them that their input is valued, which can boost morale and job satisfaction.

Lastly, don't be afraid to revisit your processes regularly. What works today might not work tomorrow, especially as your business grows or as industry standards shift. Make process improvement an ongoing effort, not a one-and-done task. Set aside time every quarter to review what's working, what's not, and what needs tweaking. It's like maintaining a well-oiled machine—regular tune-ups keep everything running smoothly.

By continually refining your processes, you're not just improving the quality of your work—you're also setting yourself apart from the competition. In a crowded market, the businesses that thrive are the ones that never stop striving to be better.

STANDING OUT IN A COMPETITIVE MARKET

PRICING YOUR SERVICES STRATEGICALLY

You already know your craft inside out and deliver top-notch work. But here's an uncomfortable truth: being good at what you do isn't enough. If your pricing is off, you risk either leaving money on the table or scaring away the clients you want. Strategic pricing isn't just about numbers; it's about positioning, perception, and profitability. Let's break this down so you can charge confidently and attract the right clients.

Understanding Market Rates and Margins

Pricing is part art, part science. The first step is knowing the market rates in your area—not just guessing, but actually doing your homework. What are other electricians charging for similar services? Are they charging per hour, per job, or offering flat rates? You can find this information by talking to other tradespeople, checking industry forums, or even mystery-shopping competitors.

Once you have a sense of the local going rates, don't make the mistake of blindly copying them. Your goal isn't to match the competition; it's to understand where you fit in the market. Are you the premium option with high-end expertise and white-glove service? Or are you offering no-frills, reliable work at a budget-friendly price? Where you position yourself will dictate your pricing.

Then, factor in your costs. Many small business owners un-derestimate what it really takes to keep the lights on. It's not just about covering materials and labour but also accounting for things like insurance, fuel, tools, marketing costs, and even downtime between jobs. If you're not tracking these expenses, start now. You need to know your margins to make informed decisions.

Here's a key tip: don't race to the bottom. Competing solely on price is a losing game. There will always be someone willing to do it cheaper, but cheaper doesn't equate to better. Instead, focus on delivering value that justifies your price.

Offering Value-Driven Packages

Let's get real: most customers don't just want a service—they want a solution. And they want to feel like they're getting more bang for their buck. That's where value-driven packages come in.

Think about the services you offer and group them into bundles that make sense for your clients. For instance, if you do domestic electrical work, you could create a "Home Safety Package" that includes a smoke alarm check, electrical safety inspection, and light fixture upgrade. If your niche is commercial properties, you might offer a "Business Continuity Package" that includes emergency lighting testing, backup generator maintenance, and a wiring health report.

By bundling services, you're not only increasing the perceived value but also encouraging clients to spend more with you in one go. This approach also simplifies decision-making for your customers. Instead of picking and choosing individual services, they see a clear, all-in-one solution that meets their needs.

When you present your packages, focus on the benefits, not just the features. A homeowner doesn't care that you're using a specific brand of smoke alarm—they care that their family will sleep safer at night. A business owner isn't impressed by technical jargon about wiring—they care that their operations won't grind to a halt because of an unexpected power issue. Always lead with the "why" behind your offer.

And don't be afraid to create tiered options. For example:
- Basic Package: Covers the essentials at a competitive price point.
- Standard Package: Adds a few extras that most clients value.
- Premium Package: The works—perfect for clients who want everything taken care of, hassle-free.

By offering multiple options, you give customers control over how much they want to spend while anchoring their perception of value. Many will choose the middle option, but having a premium tier positions your brand as capable of delivering high-end results.

Knowing When to Adjust Your Prices

Pricing isn't static. As your business grows, your expertise sharpens, and your reputation builds, your prices should reflect that. But raising rates can feel daunting—what if you lose clients?

Here's the thing: not all clients are created equal. If someone balks at a small price increase, they're likely not your ideal customer. Your goal is to work with people who see the value you bring and are willing to pay for it.

When raising your prices, timing and communication are key. First, give your existing clients a heads-up. A simple email or letter explaining the increase and why it's necessary can go a long way. Highlight any improvements in your service or added value they'll receive. For instance, if you've invested in new tools or certifications that improve the quality of your work, let them know.

Second, phase in the new rates gradually. Start with new clients while maintaining the old rates for current customers for a set period. This gives loyal clients a chance to adjust and shows you value their business.

Third, don't apologise for your pricing. You're not just charging for the time it takes to complete a job—you're charging for your years of experience, your expertise, and the peace of mind you deliver. Be confident in the value you provide.

Finally, keep an eye on market dynamics and adjust as needed. If you're constantly booked out weeks in advance, that's a sign you could increase your rates. On the flip side, if you're struggling to close deals, it might be time to revisit your pricing strategy or how you're communicating your value.

Remember, pricing isn't about being the cheapest—it's about being the best choice. When you nail your pricing strategy, you'll not only stand out in a crowded market but also build a business that's profitable, sustainable, and rewarding.

CREATING IRRESISTIBLE OFFERS

When it comes to standing out in a crowded market, one of the most effective tools in your arsenal is crafting offers that your customers simply can't refuse. The right offer not only gets people through the door but can also turn a one-time client into a long-term customer. Let's break this down into three strategies that can help you create offers that leave your competitors scratching their heads while you rake in the business.

Designing Bundled Services

Your customers don't just want a quick fix—they want solutions. Bundled services are a brilliant way to package those solutions and deliver more value while increasing your bottom line. Think about the common jobs you're already doing. Can you group them into a convenient package?

For example, if you're an electrician, instead of just installing a ceiling fan, why not offer a "Summer Comfort Bundle" that includes the fan installation, an electrical safety inspection, and a discounted rate on upgrading outdated outlets? You're not only giving your customer more value but also positioning yourself as someone who looks out for their long-term needs.

Bundling services also gives you an opportunity to up-sell without coming across as pushy. A homeowner may call you for something straightforward like installing a new light fixture, but when you offer a "Home Lighting Upgrade Package" that includes dimmer switches, energy-efficient bulbs, and smart controls, they're likely to see the benefit in doing a bit more while you're already there.

The key to successful bundling is to focus on convenience and relevance. Your customer should feel like they're getting an all-in-one solution that saves them time, money, or both. Think about the pain points your clients face—whether it's safety concerns, rising energy bills, or outdated systems—and then create packages that solve those problems.

Make it even more enticing by adding a limited-time bonus. For example, "Book the Summer Comfort Bundle by 31st August, and we'll throw in a free surge protector upgrade." That little push can be the nudge someone needs to act quickly.

Offering Limited-Time Discounts

Urgency is a powerful motivator. When people believe they might lose out on a good deal, they're far more likely to act now rather than later. That's why limited-time discounts can be so effective in driving new business.

Think about the seasonal trends in your trade. Are there certain times of year when people are more likely to need your services? If you're an electrician, you know summer is peak season for air conditioning installations and winter is a good time to promote heating system upgrades or holiday lighting installations. Use these natural cycles to your advantage by offering time-sensitive discounts that align with what your customers are already thinking about.

For example, you could promote a "Pre-Winter Electrical Check-Up" at 20% off for customers who book in October. Not only does this get you in the door, but it also allows you to identify any additional work that might need doing.

Another approach is to tie your offer to a specific event or milestone. Maybe your business is celebrating its 10-year anniversary, or you're launching a new service. Use the occasion to create a one-off discount. For instance, "To celebrate 10 years of keeping your homes safe, we're offering £50 off all electrical inspections booked this month."

The trick is to make the discount meaningful but not so steep that it eats into your profits. You still want your customers to see the value in your work. And always set a clear deadline—whether it's a date ("Offer ends 30th September") or a limit on availability ("Only the first 20 bookings will qualify"). A sense of scarcity makes people act fast.

Promoting Seasonal Specials

Seasonal specials are like the cherry on top of an already well-run business. They allow you to stay relevant, keep your name top of mind, and capitalise on the natural ebb and flow of customer demand throughout the year.

Start by thinking about the seasons and how they impact your customers' needs. For electricians, summer might mean outdoor lighting installations, while winter could be all about heating systems, electrical safety inspections, or holiday light setups.

Let's say it's springtime, and homeowners are eager to spruce up their gardens. That's your chance to roll out a "Spring Outdoor Lighting Special," offering discounted rates on garden light installations or upgrades. You're not just selling a service—you're helping people enjoy their homes in a new way.

Seasonal specials also give you a reason to reach out to past customers. Send them an email, post on social media, or even send old-school postcards highlighting your latest offer. For example, a Christmas special could be something like, "Get Your Home Holiday-Ready! Book a decorative lighting setup by 15th December for just £199."

Don't underestimate the power of holiday-themed promotions either. Valentine's Day, Easter, Halloween—these can all be opportunities to get creative. For instance, a summer promotion could be: "Stay Cool This Summer! Book an air conditioning installation by 31st July and get a free energy-efficient ceiling fan."

One of the best things about seasonal specials is they give you a natural reason to create urgency. After all, no one's going to take advantage of a "Back-to-School Energy Savings Package" in December. Use that time sensitivity to your advantage, and make sure your promotional materials—whether it's a Facebook ad, a flyer, or a post on your Google Business page—clearly convey that the offer has an expiration date.

Remember, the goal isn't just to attract new customers but to create buzz around your business. Seasonal specials make you memorable. Even if someone doesn't take advantage of your spring garden lighting offer this year, they'll remember you when they're ready to upgrade next year.

By focusing on bundled services, limited-time discounts, and seasonal specials, you can create offers that not only attract attention but also convert interest into bookings. These strategies keep you relevant, competitive, and top-of-mind for your customers—all while boosting your revenue in the process.

BOOSTING YOUR VISIBILITY LOCALLY

When it comes to standing out in your local area, visibility is the name of the game. You can be the most skilled electrician in town, but if no one knows you exist, your talents won't translate into more jobs or bigger profits. Fortunately, boosting your local visibility isn't about shouting the loudest; it's about showing up in the right places, building trust, and embedding yourself in the community. Let's explore how you can make your business the first name that comes to mind when someone needs an electrician.

Sponsoring Community Events

Getting involved in local events is like shaking hands with your entire town at once. Whether it's a school fundraiser, a sports tournament, a charity auction, or a neighbourhood street fair, these gatherings are prime opportunities to get your business in front of people who could become your next clients—or recommend you to someone who will.

To start, look for events that align with your brand values and target audience. If your niche is smart home installations, sponsoring a home improvement expo makes sense. If you specialise in energy-efficient solutions, why not support a local eco-friendly initiative? Even smaller events, like sponsoring a youth football team or donating your services to a community project, can have a big impact.

It's not just about slapping your logo on a poster and calling it a day. Engage actively. Set up a booth at the event, hand out branded merchandise (think pens, notepads, or even small tools), and be ready to chat with attendees. Offer free consultations, quick tips on electrical safety, or even a small giveaway like "win a free home electrical inspection." These interactions create a personal connection that a business card alone can't achieve.

Don't forget the follow-through. Take pictures of your involvement and share them on your social media channels. Tag the event organisers, post a thank-you message, and show off your active participation. It's a simple way to keep the momentum going, long after the event is over.

Partnering with Local Businesses

You're not in this alone. Partnering with other local businesses opens doors to a wider audience and positions you as an integral part of the local economy. Think of it as teamwork for mutual growth. The key is to find businesses that complement your services rather than compete with them.

For instance, builders, plumbers, HVAC technicians, and carpenters are all natural allies for electricians. When a builder takes on a new project, they'll need someone to handle the wiring. When a plumber installs a new water heater, they may recommend someone to ensure the electrical work is up to code. By forming partnerships, you create a network of referrals that works both ways.

Approach these businesses with a clear value proposition. Explain how you can help their customers and how they, in turn, can help yours. You might offer to bundle services—for example, a builder could include your electrical work in their project quotes—or simply agree to recommend each other when the opportunity arises.

Beyond trades, consider collaborations with less obvious but equally impactful partners. Local hardware stores could display your business cards or flyers at their counters. Appliance retailers might refer you to customers needing professional installation. Even coffee shops or gyms might let you leave a stack of brochures in exchange for helping them out with their electrical maintenance needs.

Make these partnerships public. A simple social media post like, "Excited to be teaming up with Smith's Plumbing for all-in-one home services!" can go a long way in spreading the word. It's not just about building business relationships; it's about showing your community that you're connected and trusted by other local experts.

Sending Out Direct Mail Campaigns

In an age where inboxes are overflowing and social media feeds are saturated, there's something refreshingly personal about receiving a piece of mail. Direct mail might seem old-school, but it's still one of the most effective ways to grab attention—especially when targeting homeowners in your area. The key is to do it right.

Start by crafting a message that speaks directly to your audience's needs. What's their biggest pain point, and how can you solve it? Maybe they're worried about outdated wiring, or they're interested in upgrading to energy-efficient solutions. Your message should focus on the benefits you bring—safety, efficiency, peace of mind—rather than just listing your services.

Design matters, too. A poorly designed flyer will end up in the bin faster than you can say "circuit breaker." Use high-quality images of your work, include your logo and tagline, and make sure your contact details are impossible to miss. Don't forget to add a clear call-to-action: "Call today for a free consultation!" or "Mention this flyer for 10% off your first service!"

To maximise your impact, target your mailings strategically. Focus on neighbourhoods with homes that are the right age and value for your services. If you're offering a special on EV charger installations, for instance, send your flyer to areas where residents are more likely to own electric vehicles. You can often purchase targeted mailing lists or work with local print shops that can help you refine your distribution.

Timing also plays a role. Seasonal campaigns can be particularly effective. A pre-summer mailer might focus on outdoor lighting installation, while a pre-winter campaign could highlight electrical safety checks for heating systems. By aligning your message with the time of year, you stay relevant to what your customers are thinking about right now.

Finally, track your results. Include a unique code or offer that lets you identify how many jobs came from your mailer. This way, you can refine your approach for future campaigns and ensure you're getting the best return on your investment.

Boosting your visibility locally isn't about being everywhere at once; it's about being in the right places. By sponsoring community events, partnering with other businesses, and using direct mail effectively, you'll establish yourself as a trusted, go-to electrician in your area. The more visible and engaged you are, the more your brand becomes synonymous with reliability, professionalism, and quality work. And when that happens, the jobs—and the profits—will follow.

TURNING REVIEWS INTO REVENUE

GETTING MORE 5-STAR REVIEWS

Alright, let's cut to the chase—if you're in the trades, reviews aren't just some fluffy add-on for your business. They're the lifeblood of your reputation. When a homeowner or business owner is scrolling through Google trying to decide between you and the five other electricians in their area, those little gold stars next to your name are what make all the difference. People don't trust ads; they trust other people. The more glowing reviews you have, the more you radiate trust, competence, and reliability.

But let's face it—getting customers to leave reviews can feel like pulling teeth. People are busy, distracted, and often forgetful. That's why you need a system. A process that makes leaving a review so seamless, so painless, they can't help but click those five stars and say something nice about you. Let's break down exactly how to make that happen.

Asking for Reviews the Right Way

The biggest mistake most tradespeople make is assuming their customers will just "do it on their own." They won't. Not because they don't appreciate your work, but because life gets in the way. If you want great reviews, you've got to ask for them—and ask the right way.

Timing is everything. The sweet spot? Right after the job is done. The wires are neatly tucked away, the lights are glowing, and the customer is looking at your work thinking, "Wow, this is perfect." That's the moment to strike. Don't wait a week or a month; by then, the magic has faded, and they've moved on to other things.

Here's a script you can use:

"I'm really glad you're happy with the work we've done today. It would mean a lot to me and my business if you could take just a couple of minutes to leave a quick review. It helps other people know they can trust us, and it really makes a difference. I'll send you a quick link to make it easy—would that be alright?"

Keep it simple, keep it personal, and don't sound like a robot. Most people will say yes, especially if they're genuinely pleased with the job.

Now, make it easy for them. Send a follow-up text or email with a direct link to your Google review page. If they have to hunt for where to leave a review, they'll give up before they start. Think of it like laying out the red carpet for them—click, type, post, done.

Simplifying the Review Process

You've got to make leaving a review as effortless as flipping a switch. If there's friction in the process, people won't bother.

One way to simplify things is by creating a QR code that links directly to your review page. Print it on your business cards, invoices, or even a small thank-you card you leave behind after each job. When customers scan the code, they're taken directly to the review form—no searching, no hassle.

Another pro move? Use automation tools. There are apps and software that can send review requests automatically after a job is completed. For instance, you can set up a system where, once you mark a job as finished in your scheduling software, the customer receives a personalised text or email asking for a review. Tools like NiceJob or Podium are great for this.

But here's a golden rule: don't make it all about you. Frame it as a way for them to help others. People love being helpful—it's human nature. Say something like, "Your feedback not only helps us improve, but it also helps your neighbours find a trusted electrician when they need one."

And don't forget to guide them on what to write. Most people aren't sure what to say in a review, so they either skip it or write something generic like, "Great job." While that's nice, it doesn't really sell your expertise or unique qualities. Instead, encourage them to mention specific details. For example:

- How fast you responded to their enquiry - How professional your team was on-site - How your work solved their specific problem - Any little extras you did that exceeded their expectations

The more detailed their review, the more convincing it'll be to future clients.

Responding to Reviews Professionally

Getting reviews isn't the end of the story. How you respond to them can either strengthen your reputation or chip away at it. Every single review—good or bad—is an opportunity to showcase your professionalism and customer care.

For positive reviews, don't just say, "Thanks!" That's lazy. Take a few seconds to personalise your response. Something like:

"Thank you so much for the kind words, Sarah! It was a pleasure helping you upgrade your lighting system. If you ever need anything else, don't hesitate to reach out!"

This kind of reply shows that you value your customers and aren't treating their feedback as just another tick on the board.

Now, let's talk about the not-so-glowing reviews. Negative feedback is inevitable. No matter how good you are, you can't please everyone. But how you handle criticism can actually win you more business than a dozen five-star reviews.

Step one: Stay calm. Don't take it personally, and definitely don't go on the defensive. A knee-jerk reaction can make you look unprofessional. Instead, thank the customer for their feedback and apologise for their less-than-stellar experience. Even if you think they're being unreasonable, acknowledge their perspective.

Something like: "Hi John, thank you for sharing your experience. I'm sorry to hear that we didn't meet your expectations this time. Your feedback is really important to us, and we'd like to make it right. Please reach out to us directly at [your phone number or email] so we can discuss this further."

Notice two things here: you're taking the conversation offline, and you're showing that you care about resolving the issue. Most people just want to feel heard. Even if the problem can't be fixed, your willingness to address it head-on will impress potential customers who read that review later.

And if the review is unfair or malicious? Resist the urge to fight fire with fire. Instead, respond with grace and professionalism. Future clients will see your calm, measured response and think, "This is someone I can trust if things ever go wrong."

Getting more reviews isn't just about collecting stars on Google; it's about building a reputation that makes people choose you before they even pick up the phone. With the right approach, you can turn your happy customers into your loudest cheerleaders—and that's how you win in this game.

USING TESTIMONIALS TO BUILD TRUST

When a potential client is deciding whether to hire you, they're not just looking at your qualifications or the services you offer. They're also asking themselves one big question: "Can I trust this person to do the job right?" In the trades industry, trust isn't just important—it's everything. A glowing testimonial from a happy customer can be the difference between your phone ringing off the hook and crickets in your inbox. Testimonials don't just reassure potential clients; they amplify your credibility, set you apart from the competition, and position you as the obvious choice.

Let's unpack how you can collect meaningful testimonials, showcase them effectively, and even take things up a notch with video testimonials.

Collecting Meaningful Testimonials

Not all testimonials are created equal. A generic "Great service!" won't do much to sway a new client. You want testimonials that tell a story, highlight specific outcomes, and address the exact concerns of potential customers.

Start by asking yourself: what would you want to hear if you were hiring someone? It's not enough to know a past client is happy; you need to know why. Did you solve a problem no one else could? Did you finish ahead of schedule? Did you stay calm and professional when things went sideways? These are the nuggets that resonate.

When you finish a job and you know the client is happy, ask them for a testimonial right then and there. Timing is key. If you wait too long, the details of the job—and their enthusiasm— will fade. Be specific in your ask. For instance, you could say, "Would you be willing to share a quick comment about how we helped you solve [insert specific issue]?" This helps steer them towards useful feedback without putting words in their mouth.

If a client is unsure of what to say, guide them with prompts like:- What was the problem you were facing before we worked together?- How did our service make a difference for you?- What would you say to someone considering hiring us?

This approach makes it easier for them to craft a meaningful testimonial while ensuring the focus remains on the value you delivered.

And don't forget about clients who may not be the most vocal. A quick follow-up email or text after the job is completed can work wonders. Something simple like, "Thanks for letting us take care of your [specific service]! If you're happy with the work, we'd love it if you could share a few words about your experience."

For those clients who are truly thrilled, consider going a step further. Ask them if they'd be open to a short phone interview where you can jot down their testimonial yourself. This saves them time and lets you craft a well-structured statement (with their approval, of course).

Showcasing Reviews on Your Website

Once you've collected those golden testimonials, the next step is making sure people actually see them. Think of your website as your online handshake—it's often the first impression potential clients have of your business. Testimonials should feature prominently, not buried in some obscure corner of your site.

Dedicate an entire page to client reviews, but don't stop there. Sprinkle them strategically throughout your site. For example:- Include a glowing testimonial on your homepage near your call-to-action button

- Add one or two at the bottom of your service pages to reinforce trust

- Use them in your "About Us" section to humanise your story with real-world proof.

When displaying testimonials, don't just slap up a block of text. Presentation matters. Pair the testimonial with the client's name, location, and (if they're comfortable) a photo or company logo. This adds legitimacy. A snippet like, "Tom

Davies, Homeowner in Brighton," carries more weight than just "Tom D."

If you've tackled impressive or high-profile projects, don't be shy about featuring those stories front and centre. Potential clients will naturally think, "If they handled that, they can definitely handle my job."

And here's something many tradespeople overlook: design matters. Use bold or italicised text to emphasise key parts of testimonials. Break longer ones into bite-sized quotes. The goal is to make them easy to read and impactful.

Finally, consider rotating testimonials in a slider format on your homepage. This keeps your site dynamic and ensures visitors see a variety of positive experiences without having to scroll endlessly.

Creating Video Testimonials

If a picture is worth a thousand words, a video testimonial is pure gold. Video adds a layer of authenticity that written text just can't match. People can see the client's expressions, hear their tone of voice, and feel their genuine enthusiasm. That kind of trust is hard to fake.

You don't need to be Spielberg to pull this off. A smartphone and decent lighting will do the trick. When you've wrapped up a job and the client is thrilled, ask if they'd be open to sharing their experience on camera. Keep it casual and short—no one wants to feel like they're starring in a documentary.

Guide them with simple questions like:- "What made you choose us over other electricians?"- "How did you feel about the process from start to finish?"- "What's been the biggest benefit of working with us?"

The key here is to let the client speak freely. Their authenticity is what will resonate with others. If they stumble over words or go off-script, that's fine. It makes the video feel real.

Once you've got the footage, don't just upload it raw. Trim any awkward pauses and add your logo or contact info at the beginning and end. There are plenty of free tools online that make this easy, even if you're not tech-savvy.

Post these testimonials on your website, share them on social media, and include them in email marketing campaigns. But don't stop there. If you've got a display in your office or workshop, loop them on a screen for walk-in clients to see. If you're running ads, consider using a short clip from one of your best video testimonials—it's an attention-grabber and builds trust instantly.

And here's a pro move: create a YouTube channel specifically for showcasing your video testimonials and other work. YouTube is the second-largest search engine in the world, and people searching for electricians in your area might just stumble across your glowing reviews.

By collecting meaningful testimonials, showcasing them effectively on your website, and leveraging the power of video, you're not just building trust—you're creating a snowball effect. Every happy client becomes an advocate for your business, helping to attract more of the customers you want.

HANDLING NEGATIVE FEEDBACK

Negative feedback. Nobody likes it, but it's inevitable. Even if you're the most skilled electrician in your area, delivering flawless work every single time, you'll eventually encounter a less-than-glowing review or an unhappy customer. Maybe someone misunderstood your pricing, or perhaps their expectations were out of alignment with the reality of the job. Whatever the reason, how you handle negative feedback can make or break your business. It's not just about damage control—it's about turning adversity into an opportunity to strengthen your reputation and refine your processes. Let's break it down into actionable steps.

Staying Calm and Professional

The first rule of handling negative feedback is simple: don't take it personally. It's easy to feel attacked when someone criticises your work or service, especially when you've poured your sweat into the job. But letting emotions drive your response will only escalate the situation. Instead, take a breath, step back, and approach the feedback with a problem-solving mindset.

Start by listening—really listening. If the feedback is delivered in person or over the phone, let the customer speak without interrupting. Most people just want to feel heard. Same goes for online reviews. Don't jump straight into crafting a response; read the review carefully, and try to understand exactly where the customer is coming from. What are they upset about? Is it something you can fix or improve?

When you do respond—whether online or face-to-face—keep your tone calm, professional, and empathetic. Acknowledge the customer's feelings without immediately jumping to defend yourself. Here's an example:

"Thank you for bringing this to our attention. We're sorry to hear you weren't satisfied with the service, and we'd like to understand more about your experience so we can make it right."

Notice what's missing? No excuses, no defensiveness, no finger-pointing. Just an honest, professional acknowledgment that the customer's concerns matter.

If the feedback is public, like on Google or Facebook, remember that your response isn't just for the unhappy customer—it's also for everyone else who stumbles across the review. Potential clients are watching how you handle criticism, and a measured, professional response can demonstrate your commitment to customer satisfaction. It's your chance to show you care, even when things don't go perfectly.

Turning Complaints into Opportunities

A complaint might feel like a punch to the gut, but it's also a goldmine of information. Every piece of negative feedback is a clue about where your business can improve. Didn't explain your pricing clearly enough? Maybe it's time to revise your quotes to make them more transparent. Customer felt ignored after the job? That's a nudge to improve your follow-up process.

Start by analysing the feedback. What's the root cause of the problem? Is it a one-off situation, or does it point to a recurring issue? If one customer complains about a miscommunication, it might be an isolated incident. But if several customers are saying the same thing, that's a pattern you can't afford to ignore.

Once you've identified the issue, take action. Fix the problem, but don't stop there—go the extra mile to show the customer you're serious about making things right. If you missed a deadline, offer to waive part of the fee or provide a small discount on their next service. If the issue was a misunderstanding, take the time to explain and ensure they feel valued.

Here's the thing: people don't expect perfection. What they do expect is accountability. When you own up to mistakes and take genuine steps to resolve them, you're not just salvaging a relationship—you're building trust. And trust is your most valuable currency in this line of work.

Sometimes, resolving a complaint can even turn a critic into a raving fan. A customer who starts off angry but sees you go out of your way to fix the issue might just end up recommending you to their friends and family. It's not uncommon for a well-handled complaint to turn into a glowing 5-star review.

Learning and Improving from Criticism

Once the dust has settled, it's time to reflect. Negative feedback isn't just about that one customer—it's about your business as a whole. Use it as a tool to identify blind spots and refine your operations.

Start by asking yourself some hard questions:

- Was there a breakdown in communication? - Did the team deliver the quality of work you promised? - Are your systems and processes as solid as they should be? - Did you set clear expectations with the customer from the start?

It's also worth involving your team in this process. Gather your crew and discuss the feedback openly. What could have been done differently? How can you all work together to ensure the same issue doesn't crop up again? Turning negative feedback into a team project reinforces your commitment to continuous improvement and gets everyone on the same page.

Sometimes, the problem isn't with your work or processes but with how you present your services. Misaligned expectations are a common culprit behind unhappy customers. If someone thought a job would take a day but it actually required three, it's not because you're slow—it's because they didn't understand what was involved. This is where clear communication and setting realistic expectations upfront can save you a world of headaches later.

Finally, make it a habit to document what you've learned. Create a feedback log where you track complaints, resolutions, and the changes you've implemented as a result. Over time, this becomes a valuable resource for spotting trends and making informed decisions about how to improve your business.

Negative feedback isn't fun, but it's part of the game. And here's the truth: the tradespeople who thrive long-term are the ones who embrace it, learn from it, and use it as a stepping stone to become even better. You've got this.

MARKETING ON A SHOESTRING BUDGET

FREE AND LOW-COST STRATEGIES

Let's face it—marketing can feel like a black hole for your wallet. You've got tools to buy, jobs to quote, and clients to keep happy. The idea of dropping thousands on flashy campaigns or hiring a marketing agency probably feels about as appealing as rewiring a dodgy fuse board in the pouring rain. Here's the good news: you don't need a fat budget to get your name out there. You just need to get scrappy and maximise what's already within your grasp.

Leveraging Word-of-Mouth Referrals

You're already sitting on one of the most powerful marketing tools in existence: your happy customers. People trust recommendations from friends and family more than any

Instagram ad or Google search. If you solve someone's electrical nightmare with skill and professionalism, they'll happily sing your praises—provided you give them a gentle nudge.

Start by making it ridiculously easy for clients to refer you. After you've wrapped up a job and double-checked everything's working flawlessly, simply say, "If you know anyone who needs an electrician, I'd really appreciate you passing along my details." Keep it natural. No hard sell.

Take it a step further by offering referral incentives. For instance, you could give customers a discount on their next service for every new job they send your way. Even something as small as a £10 gift card or a handwritten thank-you note can go a long way in showing your appreciation and keeping your name top of mind.

Don't forget to keep track of referrals. Whether it's a quick spreadsheet or a note on your phone, make sure you know who's sending work your way. Over time, you'll notice your most loyal advocates—these are the people you'll want to reward the most.

Making the Most of Social Media

Social media isn't just for influencers and viral dance videos. For tradespeople, it's a free stage to showcase your work, connect with your community, and build trust with potential clients. The key is to approach it with purpose rather than posting randomly whenever you remember.

Start by choosing platforms where your clients are likely to hang out. For electricians, Facebook and Instagram are usually a solid bet. Facebook is great for connecting with local communities through groups and business pages, while Instagram lets you show off the visual side of your work—like that spotless consumer unit install or the sleek lighting setup you just completed.

Consistency is more important than quantity. Post two to three times a week to keep your audience engaged without overwhelming them. Share before-and-after photos of jobs (with your client's permission), quick tips for homeowners, or even a short video explaining common electrical issues. Keep it authentic—people want to see the real you, not some polished corporate persona.

Don't overlook the power of local Facebook groups. These are goldmines for small businesses. Join groups for your town or city and keep an eye out for people asking for recommendations. When someone's looking for an electrician, jump in with a friendly comment and let them know you'd be happy to help. Just make sure you follow the group's rules—spamming will get you booted faster than a tripped RCD.

And if you're comfortable experimenting with ads, even a small budget—say £50 a month—can make a difference. Target local areas and focus on simple, clear messaging like: "Need an Electrician You Can Trust? Call [Your Business Name] Today!" Test different approaches and see what sticks.

Creating DIY Marketing Materials

You don't need a high-end graphic designer to create professional-looking materials. These days, tools like Canva make it easy to design everything from business cards to flyers to social media posts, all for free or for a small monthly fee.

Start with your business cards. They're still one of the most effective tools in your arsenal. Make sure yours includes all the essentials: your name, business name, phone number, email, website, and any relevant certifications. If you've got a memorable tagline, throw it on there too. Always keep a stack in your van—hand them out liberally, whether you're at a local café, a trade supplier, or chatting with someone at a job site.

Next, think about flyers or door hangers. These are especially useful if you're targeting a specific neighbourhood or estate. For example, if you've just completed work in a new-build development, leave a flyer in the letterboxes of nearby homes offering a discount on first-time bookings. Highlight services that resonate with homeowners, like socket upgrades, lighting installations, or electrical inspections.

Another low-cost idea: branded stickers or magnets. People love practical items they can stick on their fridge or toolbox. Include your logo, phone number, and website, along with a clear call-to-action like "Call Today for Fast, Reliable Service!" These small gestures keep your name visible when someone has an electrical issue down the line.

Finally, don't underestimate the power of your van. Your vehicle is essentially a moving billboard. Invest in magnetic or vinyl signage with your branding, contact info, and a short tagline. Keep the design simple and legible from a distance—think bold letters, clear colours, and no overcrowding. Every time you park at a job site or drive through town, you're advertising your business for free.

Marketing on a budget isn't about cutting corners—it's about getting creative with the resources you already have. When you focus on referrals, social media, and DIY materials, you'll find that you don't need a massive budget to make a massive impact.

CROSS-PROMOTIONS THAT WIN

When it comes to growing your electrical business without blowing your budget, there's a goldmine right under your nose: cross-promotions. Partnering with other businesses that complement your services isn't just cost-effective—it's strategic. You already know your customers need more than just wiring fixes or fuse box upgrades, so why not team up with other professionals who can help you serve them better while growing your own client base? It's a win-win that takes minimal investment and delivers maximum impact.

Partnering with Complementary Businesses

Start by identifying businesses that naturally align with what you do. Think plumbers, HVAC specialists, builders, roofers, landscapers, or even interior designers. These are people who are already in homes and businesses where your services could be needed. For example, if a contractor is renovating a kitchen, they'll likely need to upgrade the electrical work. Why shouldn't you be their go-to electrician?

To make this work, focus on building genuine, reciprocal relationships. You're not just looking for a quick lead; you're aiming for a mutually beneficial partnership. Start by reaching out to local businesses and introducing yourself. Don't over-complicate it—sometimes, all it takes is a phone call or even dropping by their office with a professional introduction and a handshake. Offer mutual referrals: "If you send work my way, I'll send work your way." Simple.

Take it a step further by creating bundled packages. Let's say you partner with a kitchen remodelling company. You could offer a "Kitchen Transformation Package" that includes both the remodelling and the electrical upgrades. Bundled services like this make it easier for customers to say yes because it simplifies their decision-making. Plus, it positions you as part of a team of trusted experts.

Don't forget about local retailers and suppliers. Partner with lighting showrooms, hardware stores, or energy-efficient appliance retailers. Offer to provide their customers with exclusive installation discounts or consultations. In return, they can recommend your services to their clients. It's not just about sharing customers—it's about creating an ecosystem where everyone benefits, including the customer.

Offering Joint Discounts

Everybody loves a good deal, and joint discounts are an excellent way to attract and retain customers. If you're working with a partner business, consider offering a small discount to clients who use both of your services. For example, if you team up with a roofing company, you could offer a 10% discount on electrical services for customers who replace their roof and need new wiring or outdoor lighting installed.

The beauty of this approach is that it doesn't cut into your profits as much as you might think. A slight discount is often enough to sway a customer towards choosing your service over a competitor's, especially if they're already spending money on a big-ticket item like a home renovation or a new roof.

You can also get creative here. What about offering seasonal promotions? If your region experiences harsh winters, pair up with a heating specialist and roll out a "Winter Warmth Package." This could include electrical safety checks for space heaters, heating system upgrades, or even the installation of smart thermostats. Customers appreciate businesses that anticipate their needs, and seasonal offers make your services feel timely and relevant.

Another angle is to work with businesses in completely different industries that still serve your target audience. For instance, partner with a local car dealership. How? Offer a free electrical safety check for their clients who are also homeowners. In return, they can promote your services to their customers. It's unexpected, but it works because you're tapping into a shared audience.

To make joint discounts really shine, ensure both you and your partner business promote the offer consistently. Use flyers, social media, email newsletters, and even in-store signage to spread the word. The more visible the offer, the more traction you'll get.

Sharing Audiences on Social Media

Social media isn't just a place to post project photos; it's a powerful networking tool. Partnering with other businesses to share audiences on platforms like Instagram, Facebook, or LinkedIn can significantly amplify your reach without costing you a penny.

Start by collaborating on content. Let's say you've partnered with a plumber. You could create a joint post or video showcasing a project where you both worked together. Maybe it's a home renovation where the plumber handled the pipes while you installed modern, energy-efficient lighting. Tag each other in the post, and suddenly you're in front of their followers, and they're in front of yours.

Take it up a notch with social media takeovers. This is where you temporarily "swap" accounts with your partner business for a day or even just an afternoon. During the takeover, you can showcase your work, share tips, or even go live to answer questions. It's a fun way to introduce yourself to their audience while keeping things engaging.

Another approach is to co-host online events. Imagine hosting a live Q&A session with a local HVAC specialist. You could cover topics like saving on energy bills or upgrading to smart home systems. By combining your expertise, you're not only providing value but also doubling your exposure.

Don't underestimate the power of shout-outs. If you've had a successful collaboration with another business, share it. Post a photo of the project and tag them, thanking them for their role. Encourage them to do the same. The more you cross-promote each other, the more both of your brands grow.

And remember, social media isn't just about promoting services; it's about storytelling. Let's say you've teamed up with a builder for a charity project, like renovating a community centre or fixing up a local school. Share the progress on social media, tagging your partner and highlighting the impact of your work. Stories like these resonate deeply with audiences and build trust in your brand.

When sharing audiences on social media, consistency is key. Don't just post once and forget about it. Make cross-promotion a regular part of your social media strategy. The more your audience sees you collaborating with other trusted businesses, the more credible and connected you'll appear.

Cross-promotions are more than just a clever marketing tactic—they're a way to build relationships and create a network of trusted professionals who elevate each other. When done right, they don't just grow your business; they make your brand part of a larger community that customers trust and turn to. And all it takes is a little initiative and collaboration to get started.

TRACKING ROI WITHOUT SPENDING BIG

Let's be honest—when you're running a small electrical business, every pound matters. Marketing might feel like a luxury expense, especially when you're on a tight budget. But here's the truth: you can't afford to NOT know if your marketing efforts are working. Tracking your return on investment (ROI) doesn't have to involve expensive tools or complex reports. It's about making sure every penny you spend on marketing brings more value back to your business. The good news? There are free and low-cost ways to do it that are simple, effective, and built for people like you—electricians, tradespeople, and small business owners rolling up their sleeves every day.

Using Free Analytics Tools

You don't need to hire a data scientist or spend thousands on fancy dashboards to track how your marketing is performing. Start with the tools already at your fingertips—most of them are free and surprisingly powerful.

Begin with *Google Analytics*. If you've got a website (and you really should by now), Google Analytics is your best mate for understanding how people find and interact with your site. Want to know how many people visited your services page last week? Done. Curious which of your blog posts is driving the most traffic? Sorted. The beauty of Google Analytics is that it doesn't just show you numbers; it shows you patterns. For example, if you notice a spike in traffic every time you post a "Quick Electrical Fix" video on Facebook, you know where to double down.

Next up: *Google My Business Insights*. If you're listed on Google (and if you're not, that's your first step), this tool helps you see how many people are finding your business through local search. You can even track how many clicks, calls, and requests for directions your listing generates. For a local electrician, this data is gold. If you're getting 50 calls a month from your Google listing, you know it's working. If it's only generating five, you've got some tweaking to do.

Social media platforms like Facebook, Instagram, and LinkedIn also offer built-in analytics—for free. They'll show you which of your posts are getting the most likes, shares, and comments.

Pay attention to these metrics because they tell you what's resonating with your audience. If a photo of you installing a high-tech smart switch gets twice the engagement of your other posts, that's a clue to create more content like it.

For email marketing, most platforms like Mailchimp or Constant Contact have free plans that include basic analytics. You can see how many people opened your emails, clicked on links, or signed up for offers. If you send out a newsletter about your winter maintenance deals and only 10% of people open it, you might need to rethink your subject line. But if 50% of readers click the "Book a Service" button, you've struck gold.

Measuring Success with Simple Metrics

Tracking ROI doesn't have to feel like studying for an accounting exam. Forget about complicated formulas and focus on metrics that actually matter to your business. Here are a few straightforward ones every electrician or trades-person should keep an eye on:

1. Lead Generation: How many new leads are coming in each month because of your marketing? This could be calls, emails, contact form submissions, or walk-ins. Keep a notebook or spreadsheet handy and record where each lead comes from. Did they mention seeing your Facebook post? Did they find you on Google? Knowing the source of your leads helps you figure out which marketing channels are pulling their weight.

2. Conversion Rate: Of the leads you get, how many turn into paying customers? If 20 people call you every month and 10 of them hire you, that's a 50% conversion rate. This number tells you two things: whether your marketing is attracting the right audience and whether your sales process is convincing enough to close the deal.

3. Customer Lifetime Value (CLV): This might sound technical, but it's dead simple. How much money does an average customer spend with you over time? If you install a £300 lighting system for a client and they call you three times a year for £100 maintenance jobs, their CLV is £600. Understanding this helps you decide how much you're willing to spend to acquire a new customer. If someone is worth £600 to your business, spending £50 on a Facebook ad to win them over is a no-brainer.

4. Cost Per Lead (CPL): Divide the amount you spent on marketing by the number of leads it generated. If you spent £100 on Google Ads and got 20 new leads, your CPL is £5. This tells you which marketing activities are most cost-effective. If your CPL from Google Ads is £5 but your CPL from a trade show is £50, you know where to focus your budget.

5. Return on Ad Spend (ROAS): If you're running paid ads, this is a key metric. Let's say you spent £200 on ads and brought in £1,000 in revenue from the jobs those ads generated. Your ROAS is 5x, meaning you earned £5 for every £1 spent. Tracking this ensures you're not just throwing money at ads but actually making them work for you.

Adjusting Strategies Based on Data

Once you've started tracking these metrics, the next step is to actually *use* the data to improve your marketing game. Numbers are only as valuable as the actions they inspire.

Let's say you notice that your Google My Business listing is driving most of your leads, while your Instagram ads are barely getting clicks. Instead of wasting more money on Instagram, double down on optimising your Google listing. Add more photos of your work, update your business description with keywords like "emergency electrician in Birmingham," and encourage happy customers to leave reviews.

Imagine another scenario: your Facebook posts featuring quick electrical tips are getting loads of engagement, but your posts about company updates are falling flat. The data is telling you to create more educational content because that's what your audience values. Start a weekly "Electrician's Tip of the Day" series and see how it performs.

If you're running email campaigns and notice that open rates are low, experiment with different subject lines or send your emails at different times. Maybe your audience is more likely to open emails in the evening after work rather than in the morning.

Don't forget to test small changes and see what works. This is called A/B testing, and it's a fancy way of saying "try two different approaches and see which one does better." For example, run two versions of a Facebook ad—one with a photo of you on the job and another with a picture of a completed project. Track which ad gets more clicks and stick with the winner.

Lastly, keep an eye on trends over time. Don't panic if one month's numbers aren't stellar—look at the bigger picture. If your lead generation has been steadily increasing over six months, you're on the right track. If it's flatlining, it's time to shake things up.

Tracking ROI without spending big isn't about having the most data—it's about having the *right* data and using it to make smarter decisions. By focusing on free tools, simple metrics, and actionable insights, you can ensure every pound you spend on marketing delivers real value to your business.

FUTURE-PROOFING YOUR ELECTRICAL BUSINESS

EMBRACING NEW TECHNOLOGIES

The trades world is shifting at a pace that would make even the most seasoned electrician pause. What worked ten years ago—or even five—might not cut it today. Technology is transforming the way homes and businesses consume electricity, and customers are looking for forward-thinking professionals who can guide them into this brave new world. If you want to stay ahead of the curve, you don't just need to adapt; you need to lead.

Exploring Smart Home Trends

Smart homes aren't science fiction anymore. They're here, and they're growing fast. From voice-activated assistants like Alexa and Google Nest to entire home automation systems, the demand for smarter, more efficient homes is skyrocketing. And guess what? A lot of this innovation needs someone like you to make it work.

As an electrician, you're in a prime position to capitalise on this trend. Homeowners don't want to just plug in a device—they want seamless integration. They want their lights, security cameras, thermostats, and appliances all working together in harmony. That's where you come in.

Start by familiarising yourself with the major players in the smart home space. Companies like Lutron, Ring, and Ecobee are leading the charge, and their systems often require professional installation. Even better, they need someone to troubleshoot when things go wrong. By becoming certified in installing and servicing these systems, you're not just doing a job—you're positioning yourself as an indispensable expert in a booming niche.

Here's the kicker: smart home tech isn't just for wealthy clients. Prices are dropping, and these systems are becoming more accessible to everyday homeowners. That means the potential customer base is vast. Whether you're installing a single smart thermostat or a fully automated system, the skill set is worth its weight in gold.

And don't overlook commercial clients. Offices, retail spaces, and warehouses are also embracing smart tech, from energy-efficient lighting systems to advanced security setups. The more you know, the more opportunities you'll uncover.

Investing in Energy-Efficient Solutions

The world is going green, and the trades industry is no exception. Energy efficiency isn't just a buzzword—it's a necessity. Customers are becoming more aware of their energy usage and are willing to invest in solutions that save money and reduce their carbon footprint. If you're not offering energy-efficient options, you're leaving money on the table.

Start with LED lighting. It's a simple swap that makes a big impact. Clients love the idea of slashing their electricity bills, and LEDs can last up to 25 times longer than traditional bulbs. But don't stop there. Solar panels, energy storage systems, and electric vehicle (EV) charging stations are all areas where you can expand your services.

EV charging is particularly worth your attention. Electric vehicles are on the rise, and with governments pushing for greener transportation, the demand for home and business charging stations is growing at a staggering rate. Offering EV charger installations can set you apart from the competition and open up a whole new revenue stream.

Here's a pro move: partner with manufacturers of energy-efficient products. Many companies offer training to electricians who want to install their systems. This not only boosts your credibility but also gives you access to exclusive tools, resources, and even client leads.

Don't forget to educate your clients. Most people don't realise the full range of energy-efficient options available to them. When you can explain the benefits—lower bills, reduced environmental impact, and even potential tax incentives—you're not just selling a service; you're empowering your customers to make smarter choices. That builds trust and keeps them coming back to you for future projects.

Adopting Advanced Tools and Equipment

If you're still using the same tools you started with a decade ago, it's time for an upgrade. Technology isn't just changing homes and businesses—it's revolutionising the tools you use every day on the job. Investing in advanced tools isn't just about keeping up; it's about working smarter, faster, and with greater precision.

Take thermal imaging cameras, for example. These nifty devices can detect electrical issues like overheating wires and overloaded circuits without you having to tear apart walls. They're a game-changer for troubleshooting and can save you—and your clients—significant time and money.

Or consider smart multimeters that connect to your smartphone. They allow you to log data, share reports with clients, and even troubleshoot remotely. These tools don't just make your job easier; they make you look more professional and tech-savvy to your clients.

Software tools are another area to explore. Scheduling apps, inventory management systems, and even augmented reality (AR) tools that help you visualise installations before you start can streamline your operations and improve your bottom line.

But here's the thing: technology is only as good as the person using it. Take the time to learn your new tools inside and out. Attend training sessions, watch tutorials, and practise until you're confident. The more comfortable you are with the technology, the more value you can provide to your clients.

Finally, don't forget about safety. Advanced tools often come with features that make your work safer, like insulated hand tools or voltage detectors with audible alerts. Investing in these isn't just about protecting yourself; it's about showing your team and clients that you take safety seriously.

In a world where technology is evolving at breakneck speed, staying ahead requires a commitment to learning and adapting. But the payoff is worth it. When you embrace new technologies, you're not just keeping up with the times—you're setting yourself apart as a leader in your field.

STAYING AHEAD OF INDUSTRY CHANGES

Keeping Up with Regulations and Standards

The trades industry is no stranger to rules, and as an electrician or trades-person, you know that regulations aren't just bureaucratic red tape—they're there to keep people, property, and businesses safe. But staying on top of these ever-changing standards can feel like aiming at a moving target. The problem is, if you're not up to date, you're not just risking fines or work recalls; you're putting your reputation on the line.

Start by making it a habit to review the latest updates from key industry bodies, such as the Institution of Engineering and Technology (IET) or your local regulatory authorities. Whether it's the latest Wiring Regulations (like the 18th Edition or updates to Part P Building Regulations), energy efficiency requirements, or health and safety practices, treat these updates like a non-negotiable checklist. Subscribe to their newsletters, join forums, or bookmark their updates page. You don't have to memorise every detail, but you do need to know what's changed and how it impacts your work.

Investing in the right training is another way to stay ahead. If new regulations come into play, be the first in your area to complete the relevant certification or course. It's not just about compliance; it's about differentiation. When your competitors are still "getting around to it," you've already mastered it. That builds trust with clients who want someone forward-thinking and reliable.

Another angle to consider is ensuring your team is on the same page. If you've got employees or subcontractors, their knowledge is just as critical as yours. Create a system where updates are shared regularly—whether through monthly team meetings, WhatsApp groups, or even a shared Google Drive with the latest guidelines and resources. And don't just send links. Break down what the updates mean for your jobs in plain, actionable terms: "Here's what's changed, and here's how we'll adapt."

Finally, don't overlook the role of technology in easing this burden. Software platforms and apps designed for trades professionals can help you stay compliant by flagging relevant updates automatically. Some even include templates or checklists to help you implement changes on the job site. These tools won't replace your expertise, but they will make staying ahead feel less like an uphill battle.

Continuing Education and Certifications

Being skilled at your trade is essential, but let's face it—it's not enough anymore. The industry is evolving, and if you're not learning, you're falling behind. Continuing education isn't just for apprentices or newbies; it's your ticket to staying relevant and competitive. The most successful tradespeople are the ones who never stop upgrading their knowledge.

Think of certifications as your secret weapon. Whether it's specialising in EV charging point installations, gaining accreditation in solar panel systems, or mastering the latest smart home technology, these qualifications not only make you more marketable but also open the door to new revenue streams. Clients love seeing those extra letters after your name—it screams, "This person knows their stuff."

But education doesn't always mean signing up for formal courses or spending hours in a classroom. There are webinars, online training platforms, and even YouTube channels run by industry experts who break down complex topics into bite-sized, actionable tips. Set aside time each week to learn something new, even if it's just 30 minutes. Bookmark a few trusted resources, and make it part of your routine—like sharpening your tools, but for your mind.

Networking is another underrated form of education. Join local trade groups, attend industry events, or participate in certification workshops. These environments are goldmines for picking up practical insights that aren't in any textbook. When you swap stories and tips with other pros in your field, you learn what's working (and what isn't) straight from the trenches.

If you're worried about cost, think of it as an investment rather than an expense. Yes, some courses and certifications come with a price tag, but the return on investment is massive. For every skill you add to your arsenal, you're expanding your ability to take on specialised, high-paying jobs. And when you market that new expertise, you're also signalling to your clients that you're not just another sparkie; you're the expert they've been looking for.

One more thing: don't just focus on technical skills. Business-related learning, like customer service or project management, can be just as valuable. After all, being a great electrician isn't just about wiring; it's about how you handle clients, manage timelines, and grow your profits.

Anticipating Market Demands

The trades industry is shifting faster than ever, and the only way to stay ahead is to keep your finger on the pulse of what's coming next. It's not enough to be reactive to trends—you need to anticipate them, prepare for them, and position yourself as the person clients turn to when they're ready to embrace something new.

Start by paying attention to where the industry is heading. Renewable energy is no longer a buzzword; it's a booming market. Demand for solar panels, battery storage solutions, and electric vehicle charging stations is skyrocketing. Energy efficiency isn't just a "nice-to-have" anymore; it's a must-have for both residential and commercial properties. If you're not already offering these services, now's the time to start exploring the training and tools you'll need to dive in.

Then there's the smart home revolution. From automated lighting systems to voice-controlled appliances, clients are looking for electricians who can do more than just install traditional wiring. They want someone who can make their home smarter, safer, and more efficient. The good news? Many of these systems aren't as complex as they sound once you've got the right training. And the best part? They often come with higher profit margins than standard electrical work.

But it's not just about new technology. Changes in building practices, energy regulations, and even consumer behaviour can impact what your clients need from you. For example, as more people work from home, there's a growing demand for dedicated home office setups with reliable electrical infrastructure. Or consider the rise in multi-generational living—more families are adding granny flats or converting garages into liveable spaces, and they'll need electrical work to match.

The key is to stay curious and adaptable. Read trade magazines, follow industry blogs, and listen to what your clients are asking for. If three clients in a month ask about solar panels or EV chargers, that's a trend worth paying attention to.

Don't be afraid to experiment with new services, either. You don't have to overhaul your entire business overnight. Start small—maybe add one new service to your offerings and see how it goes. Use social media or your website to let clients know you're expanding your expertise, and offer introductory rates to incentivise early adopters.

Lastly, collaborate with local businesses that complement your services. If you're diving into smart home installations, connect with builders or architects who specialise in modern designs. If you're focusing on renewable energy, team up with suppliers or contractors in the green building space. These partnerships not only help you stay ahead of market demands but also expand your client base without requiring massive marketing spends.

Adapt or be left behind—that's the reality of today's trades industry. But by keeping an eye on trends, investing in your education, and staying agile, you'll always be ready for what's next. The future isn't just coming; it's already here. Make sure you're prepared to lead the charge.

SETTING LONG-TERM GOALS

Planning for Sustainable Growth

Growth doesn't just happen. You don't wake up one day to find your phone ringing off the hook and your business magically doubling in size. Sustainable growth is deliberate, strategic, and—most importantly—planned. Without a clear roadmap, you're just throwing spaghetti at the wall and hoping something sticks. You need to know where you're going, how you're getting there, and what benchmarks will tell you you're on the right track.

Start with a vision. What do you want your business to look like in five, ten, or even twenty years? Maybe you want to build a team of electricians who can handle large-scale commercial projects. Or perhaps you're looking to expand into high-demand services like solar panel installation or smart home systems. Whatever it is, write it down. Clarity breeds action.

Once you've got that vision, break it down into bite-sized, actionable goals. Big dreams are great, but they can feel overwhelming if you don't chunk them into smaller, achievable steps. Let's say you want to add three vans to your fleet in the next five years. Break it down: How many new clients do you need to afford that first van? What services should you focus on to hit the profitability needed for the second van? What systems need refining to handle the increased workload without dropping the ball?

The key is to align your actions with your goals. Every decision you make—whether it's hiring a new apprentice, investing in a new tool, or taking on a particular client—should move you closer to that vision. If it doesn't, it's a distraction. Stay laser-focused.

And don't forget to measure your progress. Use a system that works for you, whether it's a spreadsheet, project management software, or even a whiteboard in your office. Track things like revenue growth, customer retention rates, and project completion times. These metrics will keep you honest. If you're not hitting your benchmarks, it's time to reassess and adjust. Growth isn't a straight line; it's a series of course corrections.

Building a Succession Plan

Let's get real for a moment: you won't be climbing ladders and running cables forever. Whether you're thinking five years ahead or twenty, there will come a time when you'll want—or need—to step back. The question is, will your business survive without you?

A solid succession plan ensures that your business doesn't just fade away when you decide to hang up your boots. It's about creating a company that can thrive without you being involved in every single decision. This isn't just for your benefit; it's for your team, your clients, and even your family.

Start by identifying key roles in your business and the skills required to fill them. If you're currently doing everything—admin, quoting, hiring, customer service—you need to start delegating. Look at your team. Who has the potential to step up? Who could you train to take on more responsibility? If you don't have the right people yet, it might be time to start hiring with succession in mind.

Next, document everything. And I mean everything. Your processes, your contacts, your pricing structures—get it all out of your head and onto paper (or into a computer). Think of it as creating a manual for running your business. This not only makes it easier for someone else to take over, but it also makes your business more valuable if you ever decide to sell.

Speaking of selling, that's another part of succession planning. Maybe your goal isn't to hand the business down to a family member or promote someone from within. Maybe you want to sell it and enjoy the fruits of your labour. That's perfectly fine, but you'll get a much better price if your business is turnkey—meaning someone can step in and keep things running smoothly without a huge learning curve.

Finally, start having those tough conversations. If you're planning to pass the business on to a family member, make sure they're on board. Don't just assume your son or daughter wants to take over. If you're grooming someone on your team, be upfront about your plans so they know what they're working toward. Transparency is key.

Creating a Legacy for Your Business

Legacy isn't just about what you leave behind; it's about the impact you make while you're still in the game. Whether you're a sole trader or running a team of ten, your business has the potential to leave a lasting mark—on your community, your industry, and even the people who work for you.

Start by thinking about the values your business stands for. Are you the electrician who always goes above and beyond, the one who's known for exceptional customer service? Are you passionate about eco-friendly solutions and helping homeowners reduce their energy bills? Whatever it is, lean into it. Your values are what make your business unique, and they're what people will remember long after the job is done.

Your legacy also lies in the relationships you build. Think about the clients who've been with you for years, the contractors who always call you first, and the apprentices you've mentored. These connections are a big part of what will define your business in the long term. Treat every interaction as an opportunity to strengthen those relationships. Word-of-mouth referrals, repeat business, and professional respect don't happen by accident.

Another way to build your legacy is by giving back. Sponsor a local football team. Offer apprenticeships to young people in your community. Volunteer your services for a charitable cause. These actions not only feel good, but they also show that your business is about more than just making money. They create goodwill that money can't buy.

Finally, think about the mark you want to leave on the industry. You've got years of experience under your belt—what are you doing with it? Maybe it's time to start mentoring younger electricians or sharing your knowledge at trade events. Maybe you write articles for industry publications or start a YouTube channel showing others the tricks of the trade. Sharing your expertise not only helps others; it cements your reputation as a leader in your field.

When all is said and done, your legacy is about more than the jobs you've completed or the money you've made. It's about the impact you've had—the clients who trust you, the team members who've grown under your guidance, and the industry you've helped shape. So start building that legacy today. You don't have to wait until retirement to make a difference.

POWERING UP YOUR FUTURE: THE NEXT STEP TO UNSTOPPABLE GROWTH

You've made it this far, and that says something about you. You're not here to settle for average. You're here because you're hungry for growth, for impact, and for the kind of success that doesn't just pay the bills but creates a life you're proud of—a business that stands the test of time. You're here because you know there's more to being an electrician or a trades-person than just wiring homes or fixing appliances. You're building something bigger. A brand. A reputation. A legacy.

The trades industry is not for the faint of heart. It's competitive, it's demanding, and it's evolving faster than ever before. But you? You've got an edge. You're the kind of person who invests in yourself and your business. You're the kind of person who understands that coasting is not an option. Every decision you make, every tool you pick up, every interaction you have—it's all part of the bigger picture. It's all part of becoming the go-to professional in your market, the name people trust, and the face they associate with quality.

Here's the reality: the world isn't waiting for you to catch up. The businesses that thrive are the ones that adapt, innovate, and stay ahead of the curve. You've got the skills to do the work—that's a given. But the real question is, are you ready to step into the role of leader, of visionary, of someone who doesn't just react to the market but shapes it? Because that's what it takes. The trades industry is ripe with opportunity, but it's also unforgiving to those who don't evolve.

Branding. Marketing. Retention. Scaling. These aren't just buzzwords—they're the lifeblood of any successful small business. But here's the thing: none of it works without action. You can read all the strategies in the world, but if you don't implement them, they're just words on a page. Real growth happens when you take what you've learned and put it into practice, even if it feels uncomfortable at first, even if it requires stepping out of your comfort zone. Because that's where the magic happens—on the other side of effort.

You've already got what it takes to succeed. The expertise. The work ethic. The drive. What you're doing now is positioning yourself to make all of that count on a much larger scale. You're going from being a trades-person who's good at their craft to being a business owner who's great at running a company. And that shift? It's not just about making more money—it's about creating a business that works for you instead of the other way around. It's about building something that gives you freedom, stability, and the ability to focus on what truly matters to you.

Your time is valuable—more valuable than you probably even realize. That's why it's crucial to work smarter, not harder. Every system you put in place, every tool you leverage, every strategy you implement—it's all about freeing up your time so you can focus on the bigger picture. It's about creating a business that doesn't crumble if you take a day off or even a week off. Because let's be honest, burnout is real, and it's not a badge of honour. It's a sign that something needs to change. And you have the power to make that change.

Think about the kind of clients you want to work with. The kind who respect your time, value your expertise, and are willing to pay what you're worth. Those clients aren't just going to show up out of nowhere. They're looking for someone who stands out—someone who communicates their value clearly, who shows up with professionalism, and who delivers beyond expectations. That's where your brand comes in. It's not just about looking good; it's about sending the right signals to the right people. It's about positioning yourself as the obvious choice in a sea of competitors.

And let's not forget about your team. If you're planning to scale—and you should be—you need people who align with your vision, who understand your standards, and who represent your brand with excellence. Hiring and training aren't just tasks; they're investments in the future of your business. The right team can help you grow exponentially, but it starts with you setting the tone. Leadership isn't about doing everything yourself; it's about empowering others to carry the torch with you.

But here's the thing: none of this happens by accident. Growth is intentional. It's the result of consistent effort, strategic planning, and the willingness to learn and adapt. It's about taking ownership of your business and recognizing that every decision you make today is shaping the future of your company. The good news? You're not alone in this journey. There's a wealth of resources, mentors, and communities out there to support you. And if you're feeling overwhelmed or unsure of where to start, that's okay. What matters is that you start somewhere.

Success in the trades isn't just about technical skills—it's about mastering the art of business. It's about understanding your market, building meaningful relationships, and delivering an experience that keeps clients coming back. It's about being proactive instead of reactive, about setting goals and chasing them down with relentless focus. And most importantly, it's about staying true to your values while embracing change and innovation.

So, what's next? The choice is yours. You can take what you've learned and let it collect dust, or you can take action. You can start small—tweak your branding, update your online presence, experiment with new marketing strategies—or you can go all in and revamp your entire approach. Either way, the key is to keep moving forward. Progress beats perfection every time.

And if you're ready to take things to the next level, don't hesitate to reach out. Sometimes, having someone in your corner makes all the difference. Whether you need help refining your brand, optimizing your marketing, or scaling your operations, I'm here to help. Visit [WEBSITE LINK] to take the first step toward building the business you've always envisioned. Let's work together to turn your goals into reality.

This is your moment. The trades industry is evolving, and you have the opportunity to lead the charge. Don't settle for being just another electrician or trades-person. Be the one everyone remembers, the one they recommend, the one they trust. The road ahead won't always be easy, but it will be worth it. Because at the end of the day, success isn't just about what you achieve—it's about who you become in the process.

Now, go out there and make it happen. Your future is waiting. And it's powered by you.

About the Author

Paul Dunn is the owner and lead electrician at P. D. Electrical Services (SW) Limited, a reputable electrical service provider based in North Devon, UK. With a commitment to high-quality work and customer satisfaction, Paul and his team offer a wide range of services, including solar and battery storage solutions, electrical installations for holiday homes, consumer unit upgrades, EV car charger installations, rewires and alterations, and Electrical Installation Condition Reports (EICRs).

Paul is highly praised for his professionalism, promptness, and meticulous attention to detail. His clients appreciate the clear and fixed pricing, the comprehensive safety checks, and the high standard of work provided by P. D. Electrical. Many reviews highlight Paul's friendly and efficient service, noting that he often goes the extra mile to ensure customer satisfaction.

For more information about Paul Dunn and P. D. Electrical, visit pdelectrical.info.

You can connect with me on:

🌐 https://pdelectrical.info

Also by Paul Dunn

Paul Dunn, an experienced electrician and owner of P. D. Electrical, is also a prolific author who shares his expertise through various books. While many of his works focus on providing valuable insights and practical guidance for homeowners, apprentices, and professionals in the electrical field, Paul's interests extend far beyond the trade. He has authored books on a variety of topics, including AI, quantum phenomena, and self-improvement, offering fresh perspectives and actionable advice to help readers change their lives for the better.

Paul Dunn's expertise, both in practice and through his writing, makes him a trusted authority in the field of electrical services. His books are designed to empower readers with knowledge, whether they are undertaking home improvements, starting their careers, or seeking to improve their professional skills. For more information about Paul Dunn and his services, visit pdelectrical.info.

Reclaim the Power: Reclaim the Power: Capture the Sun, Control Your Energy, Conserve Your Wallet
Focusing on solar energy and sustainability, this book educates readers on how to harness solar power effectively. It covers the benefits of solar energy, how to implement solar solutions, and the financial advantages of controlling one's energy usage.

Electric Essentials: A Homeowner's Guide to Safe Wiring, Smart Upgrades, and Sustaining Property Value

A comprehensive guide for homeowners, this book addresses safe wiring practices, smart electrical upgrades, and ways to maintain and enhance property value. It serves as a practical manual for ensuring electrical safety and efficiency in the home.

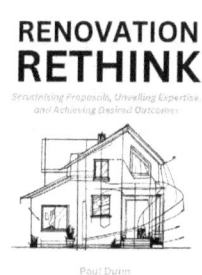

Renovation Rethink: Scrutinising Proposals, Unveiling Expertise, and Achieving Desired Outcomes

This book guides homeowners through the renovation process, emphasizing how to critically evaluate proposals, leverage expert advice, and achieve desired results. It's an essential read for anyone looking to undertake a home renovation project.

How to Electrify Your Apprenticeship: And Power Up Your Career

The first book in his Electrician's Success Path Series, aimed at apprentices and those starting in the electrical trade, this book provides career advice, practical skills, and insights into becoming a successful electrician. It covers everything from basic techniques to professional development strategies.

The Electrician's Blueprint: Navigate, Innovate & Thrive in Your Electrical Career

The second book in the Electrician's Success Path series, this book offers a roadmap for electricians seeking to advance their careers. It includes strategies for innovation, navigating the industry, and thriving as a professional electrician. It's a valuable resource for both new and experienced electricians.

Current Advances: Prepare Perfectly, Pass Professionally, Progress Positively

is the 3rd book in Paul Dunn's *Electrician's Success Path* series. This essential guide helps you confidently navigate the complexities of electrical inspections and assessments. Whether you're starting your journey or switching providers, it offers insider tips and a step-by-step compliance roadmap to ensure you pass inspections and excel in the trade. Don't let outdated practices hold you back—empower yourself with the knowledge and tools to thrive in today's fast-paced industry.

Single Quote Success: Simplify Selection, Ensure Excellence, Enjoy Peace of Mind: Why Getting 3 Quotes is a Waste of Your Time

Tired of the hassle and confusion of gathering endless contractor quotes? This book is your solution. Whether you're a homeowner or business owner, learn how to focus on quality over quantity, assess expertise, and secure the best value for your needs—all without the stress. Say goodbye to contracting frustrations and discover a simpler, smarter way to hire with confidence.

Light Up Your World: Creative Solutions for Every Room

Discover how to create spaces that inspire and energize with expert lighting tips from Paul Dunn. From layering light for depth and style to choosing fixtures and bulbs that suit every room, this guide is packed with practical advice. Learn how to save energy, solve common challenges, and master the art of illumination to make your home truly shine. Perfect for DIY enthusiasts and redesign planners alike!

Power In Numbers: How to Build a Winning Electrical Team

Paul Dunn, an experienced electrician and team leader, shares proven strategies to lead, inspire, and manage your workforce effectively. Learn how to recruit top talent, foster collaboration, balance skill development, and optimize workflows for success. Packed with actionable advice, this guide is perfect for electricians, team leaders, and business owners looking to build high-performing teams and thrive in the industry.

Rich Mind, Rich Life: Build Wealth, Overcome Obstacles & Achieving Success

Break free from financial struggles and create the life you deserve. This book provides actionable strategies to shift your money mindset, boost your income, and craft a lasting wealth plan. Unlock the tools to build wealth, conquer challenges, and live your best life. Start your journey to success today!

www.ingramcontent.com/pod-product-compliance
Lightning Source LLC
Chambersburg PA
CBHW052256220526
45471CB00001B/368